Remains of J.B. Gladney's Mill near Egypt, MS, off Hwy 8 East, north of highway on Chuauaton Chee (Chuquatonchee) Creek - picture made 1970.

Marketing in an earlier age - A wagon with a message going around the courtsquare. Sign on wagon reads "No Credit Prices. All goods charged cash prices. 10% added after 90 Days." Sign in back of wagon may be advertising a brand of butter.

"The Operating Corps" at Houston Hospital, date and identities unknown.

Sunday afternoon crowd at WCPC in Houston, 1955.

Steam engine on the loading dock on Main Street in Mantee, MS. Buildings are: Otho Hightower's Store (1); Will Scott's Store (2); bank with doctors office in back (3); and drug store (4).

Airplane that brought Houston's first "Air Mail" in 1939.

Remains of the old Enon School building, east of Houston, MS.

The old Green Tree Hotel at the Northeast corner of the square in Houston.

The old Southern Bell Telephone Office in 1955, West Washington Street, Houston.

The "Old Houston Hospital" on North Jackson Street, opened July 1920.

CHICKASAW COUNTY, MISSISSIPPI

PICTORIAL HISTORY

TURNER PUBLISHING COMPANY

ACKNOWLEDGEMENTS

The Chickasaw County Historical and Genealogical Society wishes to express our gratitude to each individual and business who contributed to this project.

Let this book be a memorial to the people who have had a part in shaping Chickasaw County, Mississippi, whether they are included in this book or remain forever faceless.

Right: Mack Priest and his brother, J.R. Priest, Jr., circa 1917.

TURNER PUBLISHING COMPANY

Publishing Consultant: Keith R. Steele
Project Editor: Charlotte Harris
Layout and Design: Beverly Ward

Library of Congress Catalog No. 2002111935
ISBN 978-1-68162-526-3
LIMITED EDITION

TABLE OF CONTENTS

THE PEOPLE OF CHICKASAW COUNTY

Hosea Abiah Wofford, born 1816, and wife Sarah E. Robertson Wofford, born 1823.

John Luke Davis and first wife, Saryan E. (Sally) Porter Knox Davis. John died in 1921, Sally in 1889.

Catherine Laughridge Craig (1814-1900) and husband Adam Kerr Craig (1800-1882).

Mary Elizabeth Pyron and William T. Smith of the Prospect Community.

W.P. Doss and father, Lemuel Doss.

Calvin Culver Lancaster

W.S. Blissard, 1807-1889. Picture made about 1864-65.

Vicie Waggoner Wooten, ca 1887, with all her children except Susie. Vicie died at Susie's birth. The children are L-R: Sallie, Anna Bell, Lula, Lizzie and Bill. Vicie was part Indian.

4

Josephine A. Martin, 1859-1893, daughter of Reuben A. and Mary Glidewell Martin. She was the wife of Elisha Monroe Sullivan, son of Dunklin and Lydia Burks Sullivan.

Eliza Emeline Hardin Neal Stringfellow, mother of Harriet F. Neal Jennings.

Mary Amanda (Bob) Faulkner Jennings, mother of Nathan Lias Jennings.

Nathan Lias Jennings, father of Rosa Jennings McQuary.

Robert Lee and Leona Corley and their children at their home in the Chalk Bluff Community, south of Okolona about 1895. Children L-R are Hubert, Jimmy, Dean, Edgar and Lee.

Andrew C. Baird Jr. (1864-1952), his wife Katie Moore Sanders and children L-R: Osma E., J.C., Gara M., Brenda Lee and Earl E.

Judge Thomas N. Martin (1807-1886), son of William and Hannah Irvin Martin, married Parthena Houser in NC and immigrated to Chickasaw County in 1836. Their daughter Nancy S. married Wm. S. Bates; their daughter Scottie, married Winfield F. Tabb.

The sons of Calvin and Nancy Hadley McGill, Steve Felix on left; Cab on the right.

Cannie Rebecca Thorn Blissard, 1879-1933, daughter of William Neal Thorn and Nancy Emily Mooneyham; wife of George Wesley Blissard.

5

John and Annie Brand Pearson with Irlene between; John, Willie and Robert in back.

The Andrew Jackson Wilson family, date unknown.

In the late 1800s, the baby is A.J. Harrington, Jr., by his mother Flora McElreath Harrington; A.D. Harrington between her and father, Andrew Jackson Harrington, Sr.. Back left is Flora's brother; back right is Callie McElreath. Flora named her sons with an "A" because she wished her sons to be first in accomplishment.

Absolum M. Cook and wife, Nancy E. Wright Cook moved to Chickasaw County in 1919 from Tennessee. Picture made 1896.

Edgar G. and Daisy Davis Coyle, grandparents of Inez Gann Dobbs.

Richard Steele Davidson (1837-1911), father of Milas Lee Davidson.

Morgan Shell, uncle of Dugan Shell, operated a mercantile store in Houston called Shell, Smith and Shell.

Dan Dulaney, husband of Minnie Tabb; father of Fred, James and Dan Dulaney.

Jep and Salley Houser Flynn, buried in the Arbor Grove Cemetery in Chickasaw County.

William Avery Pounds (1815-1902) and American Bingham Pounds (1820-1907)

Bottom row L-R: Leonard Gann (baby), Marvin Gann, Will Doss, Rachel Tedder Doss, Noah Hardin with Otis Hardin. Back row L-R: Jessie Doss Gann, Jodie Doss, Annie Doss Criddle, Jim Doss and Lizzie Doss Hardin.

D.D. (Daniel Davidson) Tabb, wife Perline Pounds Tabb with Laudie Tabb (Shell) and Catherine Shell. Made at D.D.'s home in Tabbville.

Front L-R: William Frank Higginbotham, wife Tilda Tadlock holding daughter Effie; Buren Smith Higginbotham on father's knee; Joseph Edmond Higginbotham (b. 1859) next to his wife Sarah Cordelia Georgeanna Higginbotham (they were cousins) who is holding daughter Sevella. Son Virgil is seated next. Back row L-R: ?, ?, George, Anna, Reuben Edmond and Perry.

Captain Jonothan O. Clark and wife, Cynthia Elizabeth Ann Stephen.

First row L-R: Francis Cooper Arndt, Margaret Elizabeth McGraw Arndt and sons Charles and Fred. Back L-R: Jennie Arndt Homan, Sophia Arndt Berry, Jessie Arndt House and Nancy Amelia Arndt Holiday.

Front L-R: John Elkin Smith, Sr., Cora Kilgore Smith, Sylveston Smith, Delia Carter Smith. Back row L-R: Florence Ivy Smith Harrington, John Elkin Smith, Jr., Essie Lee Smith Verell.

Tom Crumby on horse on left with his father, Dr. H.F. Crumby on the horse at right. Made in front of the Hohenlinden Store.

Eula Johnson Kimbrough and son, Hiram.

Robert Lee Brand and Evie Mayo Brand

W. P. and Rachel Doss with children Jim, Lizzie, Annie, Jessie and Jodie in front of the old Bud O'Barr house.

Seated are Dr. and Mrs. W. H. Miller of Okolona, MS, August 1900. Children are L-R: Annie (taught kindergarten and dancing in Okolona, never married), Overton Harris Miller who became wealthy from his Choctaw Culvert Co., Adelle who married for a short while and Clemintine who also never married. She lived most of her life in New York City, directing parties and tours (both domestic and foreign) for the wealthy families who wanted their children in the proper New York social circles. Clem and Annie drove to NY in their 1930 Model A Ford. The family home still stands on Prairie Street.

Sally Jane Hill Sanderson (1850-1920), wife of Hugh B. Sanderson with her children: Top L-R: Lee (1871-1941); Rosa (1874-1952) m. John H. Tabb; Robert Adolfus (1876-1908). Bottom L-R: Ida Belle (1882-1934); Dell (1879-1958) Sally and Katie Blanche (1885-1952, m. James P. Tabb, parents of J.H. and Rosalynd Tabb.

William Marion Jolly and Nancy Ann Porter Jolly, parents of Antionette, Permelia, Eliza, Elizabeth, John Lott, Waters (Wade), Christopher Columbus, Wm. Marion, James G., Marietta, and Samuel Jolly.

Nancy Rebecca McGee Johnson and husband Solomon Gilbert Johnson.

The Lude Lowery family.

Sally Higginbotham with children, L-R, Monroe, Earlene, Maylene and Richmond.

Five of six children of Jonathan and Malinda Craig Waldrop. Front L-R: Henry Franklin and Jimmie Ada; Back L-R: Mavorleen, Malinda Helen and Rebecca.

William Scarbrough (left) and Thomas Scarbrough.

James Franklin (Frank) Beaty family, 1900. Back L-R: Nena Mae (1892-1951); Joseph Franklin (Jack) 1885-1946); Eugene (1883-1947) Mary Elizabeth (Mollie) 1887-1910 and Mattie Ella (1890-1977). Front L-R: Thomas (1894-1941); Frank (1859-1935), Cary (1896-1981; Minnie Thomas (1867-1941) and baby David Augustus (Gus) Beaty 1900-1964.

Tom A. Duke, Sr., Houlka, MS, early 1900s.

Joshua Box Sullivan, born 1848.

John Armstrong and family, date unknown.

The sons of John Luke Davis and Sallie Porter. Standing L-R: Thomas Porter Davis, Jodie Lewis Davis and John Morgan Davis. Seated L-R: Lemuel Palma Davis and Malvern Hardin Davis.

Seated: Henry Womble from Woodland area and his second wife, Axis Candace Smith from the McCondy area. Standing L-R his daughter from 1st marriage, Estell; her children from 1st marriage, Henry J. and Lillie Mae Smith. Baby is their son, Roy. Made 1902.

The Ray/Finn family in 1902 or 1903. L-R: James Trenor Ray, Hattie Victoria Ray, Mary Ella Ray, Lee Andrew Ray, James Bruce Ray, Mary Elizabeth Finn Ray and Katie Irene Ray.

THE RACE/RAISH CHAPMAN FAMILY

Race/Raish Chapman was born January 1861, probably in Indiana. The first evidence of him being in Mississippi is the 1880 census where he was living with the Jud Thomas family, listed as being a farm laborer. Two houses away lived Wiley Dunson and his family, including 11 year old Roda. On May 21, 1882, Raish and Roda were married in Chickasaw County. W.L. Walters was the bondsman and they were married by A.J. Seal, a minister of the gospel.

Raish Chapman, 1861-1921

Roda Mae Dunson Chapman, 1867-1904

Jodie Walls Chapman, 1899-; Dorinda Chapman, 1981-; Dennis Chapman, 1921-

Raish and Roda lived in the "flatwoods" area of Chickasaw County. They were the parents of eight children: Adeline (1883), Mary Etta (1888), Nancy Mae (1890), Junie L. (1891), Laura Josephine (1894), William Bascom (1897), James Benjamin (1899) and Tony Eugene (1902). Roda died in 1904 and was buried in Wesley Chapel Cemetery.

On December 28, 1917, Raish married Miss Jodie Walls. She was the daughter of Josephus Andrew Walls and Harbert Ann Mathis. Jodie was 18 at the time of their marriage and Raish was 56. They were the parents of two children; Dorinda Lavon (1918) and Dennis Raish (1921). Raish died in 1921 and was buried at Wesley Chapel.

Adeline married Charlie McClung. They were the parents of five children; Marion, Lee (daughter), Jim, Billie and Hilda. The McClung's left Mississippi shortly after their marriage and moved to Arkansas where they both died.

Mary Etta had a son, Raymond Caneth, born 1905. Later she married Plumb Mathis (Harbert Ann's brother) and they had a daughter, Rhoda Mae, born 1921. Mary Etta lived her whole life in Chickasaw County, the last years being spent in Pyland. She died in 1963 and is buried in Hillcrest Cemetery in Vardaman, Mississippi.

Nancy Mae married Elbert Walls (Jodie Walls' brother) and they raised a large family. Their children; Esard O'neal, Dewight (Bud), Ruby Mae, Raymond Raish, James Durell, Kenneth Eugene, Hilda Ruth and Etta Jean. Nancy Mae died February 26, 1949, and is buried in Carroll County, Mississippi.

Junie L. died young, probably buried at Wesley Chapel.

Laura Josephine married Cluff Sims McCluney. Their children: Cora Eileen, Mary Eta and Cluff Sims (C.S.) McCluney, Jr.. Laura died August 13, 1948, and is buried in Rhodes Chapel Cemetery.

William Bascom married Grace Cobb and they had the following children: Mildred, Helen, William Bascom (Giggs), Jr.

Adeline, 1883-19

Mary Etta (left), 1888-1963 and Laura Josephine, 1885-1948

Nancy Mae, 1890-1949, and Elbert Walls

William Bascom, 1897-1989

and Freida. Bill died in 1989 and is buried in Yazoo County, Mississippi.

James Benjamin married Patty Duke. They made their home around the Greenwood, Mississippi, area. They had a large family which included Bob, Ben Jr. and Ray. Ben died in 1976.

Toney Eugene married Ruby Walls Ferguson (Harbert Ann Mathis' granddaughter). Ruby was married first to

James Benjamin, 1899-1976

Toney Eugene, 1902-1976

Wiley James, 1895-1967

Bailey Clardis Ferguson and they had two children; Martha Jo (1944) married first Walter Stewart Paden. They had one child, Michael Anthony. Mike has one daughter, Cathy Jo. Martha then married Raymond Owen and they have two children; Raymond Bradley and Brandy Nicole. Larry Lavoy (1947) married first Melba Harmon. They had two children; Larry Jr. and Lisa Michelle. He next married Cathie Hutchins and they have two girls; Chastity Lavon and Charity Elizabeth. Ruby and Toney had 10 children; Brenda Kay married first Bobby Doss Huffman and had two sons; Michael Shane and Brent Chapman. Shane married Beverly Butler and they have two sons; Michael Chase and Johnathon Wayne. Brent married Amy Hardin and they have a son named Bobby Dalton. Brent has a daughter named Sarah Alexandra. Brenda and Bobby were divorced and she married Seferino Villarreal. They have two children; Nikki Rene who married Mark Anthony Hancock and Cory Delaine. Nikki and Mark are the parents of two sons; Luke Anthony and Eli Chapman. Cory is unmarried. Regenia Darnell married first Sammy Clark Williams and they had two sons; Chad Clark and Jeremy Eric. Chad married first Lisa Denham and had a daughter Samantha Leigh. They divorced and he married Kim Morgan and they have a son Chad Clark Jr. (C.J.). Sammy died and Reginia married Caroll David Morgan. They have a son named David Raish. Pamela Ann married first Tommy Black and they had two sons; Marty Scot and Tony Andrew. Marty married Brandy Watson and they have one child Danielle. Tony married Leigh Ann Rogers and they have one child, Kristen. Pam and Tommy divorced and she married Leon Morris, no children. He has two children, Nikkie and Roger Morris. Toney Eugene married Sandy Russell and they had two children; Amanda Dawn and Alicia Rena. Toney died in 1986 and is buried at Wesley Chapel. Amanda married Drew Costin and they have three children; Jordan, Madison and Anna. Alicia married Dallas Brand and has one son, Hunter. Nancy Gail married Aaron Bray and they have three children; Tony Sheldon, Jon Aaron and Georganna. Sheldon has one child, Ethan. Judy Faye married Jackie Alexander and has two boys; Joey Lee and Jared Baxter. Joey has a son named Joseph. Cynthia Lynn married Billy Owen, no chil-

dren. Danny Joe is unmarried. James Harvey died at birth. Dorinda Rena married Tim Brown and they have one child; Derrek Matthew.

Dorinda Lavon married Carnice Tutor and they had three girls; Helen Lavern, Deloma Jean and Phyllis Diane. Helen married Laderl Washington. Their children; Gary Laderl married Lori Winters Jefferys. They have two children; Sean Jefferys and Chastin Chase Washington. Barry Greg married Edie Britt and they have two children; Whitney Eden and Haley Kim. Jeffrey Carl Washington married Karen Sappington Edwards who had two children; Shelby Edwards and Jacob Edwards. Jennifer Kim married Tim Holladay and they have two sons; Nathan Lance and Landon Wade. Deloma married Brother Junior Rithie and they have three children; Marty Chris married Jeaninne Smithson and they have two children; Ethan and Jade. Gina Marie married Bill Morgan and they have a child, Hannah. Mark Anthony married Betsy Bryant, no children. Phyllis married Kent Anderson. Their children; Chad married Cammie Bussy, one child, Nicholas. He married second Kelly Linley and she has one child, Taylor. Amy married Keith Holladay and they have one child, Olivia. Jody married Allison and they have one child, Walker. Felicia married Jason Putt, no children.

Dennis Raish married Artleen Ferguson. Their children; Carolyn Jane married first Rayburn Swanson and had three girls, Myra, Rhonda and Paula. Carolyn then married Greg Stewart and they have one daughter Leigh Ann. Jerry Raish married first Shelby Brown. Their children; Jerry Michael, Marsha Rena and Jeffery Scott. He next married Susan Jackson and they have one son, Shane Raish. Margo Elizabeth married Jimmy Dodson. They have two children; Susan Michelle and Christopher Lee. Rita Darlene married James Huckaby, no children. David Allan married first Darlene Brown, one child, Selina. Next married Cora Garrett and has one child, Jessica Renee. Catherine Darnell married Terry Loggins and they have two sons; Jeremy Howard and Jayson Raish.

Raish Chapman was the father of another son, Wiley James Dunson. Wiley was born July 3, 1895, and died in 1967. He is buried in Fletcher's Chapel Cemetery in Yazoo County, Mississippi.

Daniel "Foster" Wilson, (1886-1956); date of picture unknown.

Clara Florence Hadley Davidson (1878-1961) wife of Milas Lee Davidson.

H.N. Harbin, 1832-1916, lived in Chickasaw County from mid to late 1800s.

Samuel Jackson Nabor (died 1912) and Sarah Hasentine Gray (died 1933); great-grandparents of Gordon Huffman.

Crawford Gilliam Neal, born February 21, 1840, buried Friendship Cemetery.

Georgia Avent Newell, wife of A.A. Newell, taught at Houlka School for many years.

A.A. Newell, second principal at Houlka School. Also taught at Banner, Pittsboro, and Coffeeville. He also served as Mayor of Houlka several times.

Sarah Spencer Thomas, second wife of Richard Thomas.

Mattie Houser, mother of George Jackson Houser.

Back row L-R: John Brand, Annie Brand Pearson, Betty Brand, Jim Brand, Lee Brand, Billy Couch, Maggie Couch Brown, Ben Couch, Kitty Couch Parker and Bob Couch. Front L-R: Henry Couch, Vada Couch Earnest, Ed Couch, Ruth Couch Cox, Molly Cox Thacker, Betty Cox Brown, Annie Cox Huffman, D.L. Cox and Hill Cox.

Garland H. (Dick) Anderson (1873-1948) and Rebecca (Lee) Anderson (1874-1952). Married in 1895, their children were Charles Wm. Anderson (1895-1982); Dewey Hobson Anderson (1898-1941); Mavis Claire Anderson Corley (1902-1975); Mary Shaw Anderson, (b and d 1904); Garland Haden Anderson (1905-1985) and Hadie Alaine Anderson (1907-1982). Rebecca was the dau. of Alex and Mary Lyon Lee of Virginia.

L-R: John J. Dye and Dunklin M. Sullivan, grandfathers of Nannie Sullivan Cook who is holding Tura Cook Jernigan, Carl Cook and son Eugene in front. Made in 1906.

John Lee Gaskin and Edna Earl Jolly Gaskin with daughters, l-r: Mary Ann Gaskin Sullivan and Lessie Gaskin Fike; baby Leon Gaskin and son (standing) Howard Gaskin. Four of nine children. Picture made early 1906.

Henry Monroe Skelton's family, ca 1906. Claude, Blondie, Henry and Inez (baby), Nora, John Abb, Price and Martha Hays Skelton.

Modera Malinda Verell Wilson and husband Daniel Foster Wilson with their first born, Lex Byron Wilson. Picture made late 1906 or early 1907.

Emma C. Moore Jemison (1879-1910), first wife of William Edward (Luck) Jemison (1877-1954). Children from L-R: Lottye Beatrice 1901-1971; John Wilkinson Jemison 1899-1957; William Homer Jemison 1905-1981; Robert Aldwin Jemison 1902-1957. Circa 1907, Sparta.

Charles Franklin Wilson and wife, Minnie Rhodes Wilson with children (L-R) Harold, Ethel, Irene and Clarence. Photo made about 1907-08.

Jesse Lee Guinn and Frances Ulmer Guinn family. Bottom L-R: Mark, Lula Mae, Jesse Lee and Frances. Back L-R: Elias (Buddy), Ulmer, Maggie and Hurd.

Tessie Mary Vaughn Martin, Robert Lee Vaughn, Ishmael Lee Vaughn, Mary Allena (Lena) Grissom Vaughn, Joseph Augustus Vaughn and Zelma Viola.

The Parker family, first row, L-R: William David, Vardaman, Ruby, DeHay. Second row, L-R: C.L., P.S., Clarence, Clara, Lucretia "Creeta."

L-R: Austin M. (Aut) Martin, Jackson Van Buren Martin, his wife Roseltha A.M. Lowrey Martin, his daughter Minnie Lee Martin Roebuck, Mattie A. Johnson Martin and Eddie Smith Martin; the dog is "Old Lady Bird Dog."

Sons of B.C. Lancaster, circa 1907-08. Back: left-Allie Lancaster, center-Hobson Lancaster, right-Winifred Lancaster. Front left is Dulin Lancaster and baby is Eldridge Lancaster.

Children of Alured Dehillard and Margaret Frances McKee Lowery. Front L-R: Rachel Manerva Lancaster, Mary Catherine Moore, Martha Della Helms, Etta Hylann Walters. Back row L-R: John Andrew, Margaret Zelda Wooldridge, Pearlie Ethel Smith, Henry Lawrence.

Home of B.C. Lancaster, before October 1909. Back row, L-R: Lon Neal, Bernie Lancaster Neal, Mamie Lancaster, Nettie Lancaster, Luther Lancaster, Lena Wilson Lancaster. Middle row, L-R: (horse is Walker), Calvin Culver Lancaster, Hobson Lancaster, (dog is Bradford), B.C. Lancaster, Molly Foster Lancaster and Allie Lancaster. Seated in front is Winifred and Dulin Lancaster.

A.K. (Alfred) Mixon

In the Concord Community abt. 1909. Front L-R: Minnie Joe Davis Seay (1878-1910), Estelle Beaty Seay (1905-1996), Bessie Mae Seay (1900-1984), Carey Elizabeth Seay (1898-1987) Grace Lee Seay (1902-1984) and William Ira Seay (1876-1935).

Jess Pettit with wife, Irene Clark Pettit, and child.

Seated L-R: Riley and Mary Martin Duncan, Sally Duncan. Children L-R: Gaston, Emma D. Grissom, Pearl D. Everett and John Duncan.

Lee Rhodes, left, and Jack Bradshaw.

Home of James Monroe Foster, L-R: ?, Molly Foster, Maggie Foster, Solomon Anderson, Ella Foster Anderson, James M. Foster, Zada Foster, Martha Louise Thompson Foster, Alice Foster, Orlando Foster, Alice Kennedrick Foster, Tiercey Foster and John Foster.

Jake and Anna Higginbotham Nabors with baby Joseph Nabors. Standing is Jake's niece, Bessie Nabors, daughter of Candy Nabors.

Levica Kimbrough and wife Emma Eula Johnson holding their son Wilburn.

Sally Ann Johnson and husband Robert Lee (Bob) Grimes with their son Pervie Lee Grimes. Made in the early 1900s.

Sidney Eiland Johnson and wife Susie Rambo

Noah C. Alford and wife Carie Mae Johnson Alford

Chester Aston and wife, Hattie Lovetta Johnson holding their baby. Hattie was the daughter of Solomon and Nancy Rebecca McGee Johnson.

Henry Clay Schwalenburg, died 1896; father of Emma Mooney-ham.

Seated is Josiah Clark, son of Joseph and Susannah Norwood Clark. Standing left to right is his second wife, Froney Foshee and his daughter Oda.

Jesse Elias Wofford (1843-1913) and wife Ellen Rebecca Gore (1839-1917) whom he married in 1873. Blinded at age 12, he became a law student at age 17 and was known as "Blind Jesse." Grandparents of Jewell Wofford Pepper and Scott Wofford.

Tom Henry Weaver (son of Andrew Weaver) with daughter Mary Elizabeth (Polly), son Ruffus Augusta (Sonny) and wife Angie Armstrong Weaver.

Mary Ann Martin King

Simpson Clark, buried in Old Town Cemetery in Calhoun County, Mississippi.

Front L-R: John and Cora Kilgore Smith; Elkin Smith. Standing L-R: Florence Smith Harrington, Essie Smith Verell and Veston Smith.

L-R: Tura Jernigan Cook, Eugene Cook, Cornelia F. Dea Tinnison, Dovie Lee Cook Floyd and Tennyson Cook.

Joseph Elias Weaver

Andrew Weaver, father of Tom Henry Weaver.

Mr. David Long with his first 3 grandchildren. L-R: Bobby Lee Gann, Esterlene Harmon Latham and Jack Harmon.

Reuben Edmond and Mary Smith Higginbotham with children Hubert and John D.

Dr. S.K. (Samuel Kirkham) Gore, (1886-1955) wife Cora Scarbrough Gore and their son Thomas M. Gore (1906-1967).

Circa 1910, Hattie Victoria Ray stands behind James Bruce Ray and Mary Elizabeth Finn Ray.

James L. (Shorty) Doss, Jessie Lee Doss and Annie Estelle Doss.

William Alexandra Culpepper, (1890-1912).

Miranda (Marianna?) Fondren Martin, wife of Austin H. Martin.

Roseltha Ann Minerva Lowery Martin (1847-1929)

Scottie Bates Tabb, date of picture unknown.

John Rufus (Buck) Canipe

Mrs. Victoria Gable, "Mrs. Vic," grandmother of Herman Smith.

William Green Skelton, 1837-1929

John and Pearl Naron Duncan

Circa 1910-1911. Seated is Calvin Culver Lancaster. L-R is Beulah Lancaster Mixon, James H. Washington Lancaster, Bo Lancaster, Absalom Dulin Newport Lancaster and Bell Lancaster Ward.

George Wesley Clark, his wife Elizabeth Jane Martin. Children L-R: Emma Irene, Florince Lorane, Lillie Ida, Audry Mae, John Wesley, Elizabeth (Lizzie), William Flenoy and Minnie Lee. Made 1913.

Family of Robert and Leona Corley, Okolona, MS, ca 1915. Front L-R: Edgar, Robert Lee, Eva (Huffman) Leona and Doy. Back L-R: George, Dean, James, Hubert, Lee and Clarence.

Jesse Franklin Criddle and family, Houston, MS, ca 1916. Front L-R: Leona Wooten, (niece of Anna Bell), Anna Bell Wooten Criddle holding Gertrude Criddle Gann; Cynthia Criddle (Kilgore); Jesse Franklin Criddle and John L. Criddle. Back row L-R: Vannie Mae Criddle (Gann); Emmitt Criddle (in front of Vannie Mae); Trannie Lou Criddle (Gann); Bryant Criddle; Chester "Chess" Criddle.

Sidney and Susie Johnson and children.

Bud and Nancy McGee and family.

George Washington Alford and Frances Irvin Alford

Shirley Hawkins Harrington and Andrew Jackson "A.J." Harrington, Jr., shortly after their marriage in 1918.

Alleene Doss and Daisey Houser

Swanza Edwin Hancock and wife Sallie Grimsley, date unknown. He was the father of James Edwin Hancock.

Andrew Jackson Wilson (1842-1923) became a POW at Vicksburg, MS, released July 7, 1865, given $7. Traveled from Vicksburg to Bellfountaine in Webster Co. to family. Later served as Supervisor from Chickasaw Co. Active in Prospect Methodist Church; grandfather of Owen Lancaster, Jewell Lancaster Jennings, Miriam Lancaster Rusico and Evelyn Lancaster Chambers.

Henry Brogan

Cluff Sims McCluney, 1872-1956, holds C.S., Jr., (b. 1917); wife Laura Josephine Chapman McCluney holds Cora Eileen McCluney Cook (b. 1919). Standing are Iris Cathleen McCluney (b. 1903) and brother Denton McCluney (b. 1902), children of his first wife, M. Rish.

James Henry Willis Walter Williams (Will Doc) and wife, Lilly Kimbrough Williams and three of their children, Etta Mae, Duette and Robert Preston Williams.

Henry Haskell Woodridge

Gordon family reunion, 1919. In the center with scarf on her head is Mary Francis Gordon and James M. Gordon. Lady in center front is Mary Alice Gordon House and her brother James Sidney Gordon.

Mrs. James M. Gordon (Mary Francis) with 7 of 8 children in 1919. L-R: Hettie House, Mary Alice House, James Sidney "Jimmy" Gordon, Tom or Hugh ? Gordon, Jeff Gordon. Back row: Hugh or Tom ? Gordon, Carrie Guest Edwards. Anna Gordon Thompson not present.

Gus Ray and Maudie Duncan Ray, parents of Betty Ray Clark.

L-R seated: Andrew Jackson (A.J.) Weed (1885-1969), his wife Pearl Mae O'Barr Weed (1890-1979) holding son James (1920-1978). Standing L-R: daughter, Alma Maie (1908-1933); A.J.'s mother Sabre C. Brown Weed (1854-1936) and daughter Annie Lou Weed.

Seven of Bedford and Laura Buggs Hobson's children. Back row standing: Oscar, Oda, Ida and Florence. First row standing: Eula; Mattie is on Bedford's lap; seated next to Laura on her lap is Lula Bell. Laura's mother, Jane is seated next to Laura.

The Charlie Park family in the 1920s.

L-R: Bolin C. Lancaster, Absalom Dulin Newport Lancaster, Beulah Lancaster Mixon, James H. Washington Lancaster and William Crofford Lancaster.

Left: Claude Johnson in the early 1920s, son of Solomon and Nancy R. McGee Johnson.

Middle: Rev. Martin C. (1879-1964) and Myrtle Abigale Weeks Putnam (1890-1972), about 1920. Rev. Putnam was a Baptist preacher and blacksmith.

Right: Mattie Naron McQuary and James Monroe McQuary.

IN MEMORY OF
JAMES LAVIRT AND VERA MAY BAILEY CLARK

Virt Clark

Vera Mae (Bailey) Clark and James LaVirt "Virt" Clark

Vera Clark

James and Glenda Clark

Robert and Dubhee Clark, Seth Clark, Jonothan Torres

Edward and Vicky Clark and Derrick Brown

Donald and Miriam Clark, Wes and Don Clark

Wes Clark

Don Clark

Childa and Fred Stevens, James and Michael Alexander

Dusty Alexander

Dusty Alexander and Mike Alexander

Idell Johnson, Myrtle Rucker and Gertrude Johnson.

Judge William S. Bates, born September 30, 1830. He married Nancy Susan Martin, daughter of Judge Thomas N. Martin. Their daughter, Scottie Bates, married Winfield T. Tabb and gave birth to W. Bates Tabb. Photo made July 22, 1922.

Benjamin Wm. Pounds, 1844-1928, and grandson, Curtis Newman Pounds in 1922. Veteran of Co B, 22 MS Regiment. Benjamin was the son of Wm. Avery and America Bingham Pounds; wife was Darthula Sims, daughter of James R. and Naomia Griffin Sims.

Odean Putnam, about 15 years old; picture made about 1925. Odean married G.C. Mabry, Jr.

Waitus-Jolly family reunion, 1925

FAMILY OF THOMAS JEFFERSON LOWRY
EARLY CIRCUIT RIDER IN CHICKASAW AND CALHOUN COUNTIES (1842-1890)

Rev. T.J. Lowry, Circuit Preacher 1890

Rebecca Farr Lowry wife of T.J. Lowry (1890)

Alfred Rushing Lowry and wife Elizabeth Doss Lowry.

Alfred Rushing Lowry and son C.D. Lowry (1924)

Fannie and Columbus Doss Lowry, son of A.R. Lowry.

Era and Thomas Jefferson Lowry, son of A.R. Lowry.

John Alfred Lowry and Fannie, son of C.D. Lowry.

Louise Motley Lowrey and E.J. Earnest, daughter of C.D. Lowry (1951)

Family of C.D. Lowry. Front: Fannie, Elizabeth Maddux, Rosemary Rhine, Chuck Rhine, Joann Houston, Louise Earnest. Back: John A. Lowry, Rosco Rhine, Ann Maddox, Bob Maddux, C.D. Lowry, Charliebeck Houston, Charlie Houston, E.J. Earnest.

Louise and E.J. Earnest 50th wedding anniversary (2001)

Family of Louise Motley Lowry Earnest: Jack William, Earvin Joseph, Louise, Joe Doss, John Edward and James Earvin (back).

Grandchildren of Louise and E.J. Earnest. Front: Stacey, Robert, Richard and Josh. Back: E.J., Jordan, Carrie, Ben, Louise and Doss.

Gordon family 1926-27. Back L-R: Walter Gordon, Josie Gordon Blue, Winfred Blue, Emmett Dendy, Anna Gordon Dendy, Elkin Dendy, Wilma Dendy. 4th - Christine Smith, Charlie Smith, Lula Smith, Lillie Bell Ferguson Gordon, Britt Gordon, Henry Gordon, Thora Stevenson Gordon, Chester Gordon, Thellie Flynn Gordon; 3rd-U.T. Gordon, Tommy Gordon, Delia Gordon, Elzie Parker Gordon, Augustus Evans Gordon. 2nd Tessie Churchman, ?, James Sidney Gordon, Hattie Dobbs Gordon, Maynette Gordon, Mim Gordon, Britt Gordon and Carl Gordon. Front L-R: Bob Gordon, Celeste Gordon, Henry "Jr." Gordon, Jack Gordon, Fred Gordon, Lorette Gordon and Eloise Gordon.

William Luther Pumphrey with wife, Susie Kate and son, W. L. Pumphrey, Jr. 1928.

Ida Lowery, Jeanette, Barney and Maxine.

Twins Lula Hill Robertson and Lila Hill Faulkner with Maylene Rish, daughter of Lula.

Standing L-R: Black Little, Clara Verell Little, Roberta Verell Sanders (face only), Ella Mae Dendy Verell, Ola Davis Verell, Charles Edward Verell, Iota Houser Verell, Gradon Verell, Essie Smith Verell and Thomas Albert Verell. Seated is Susan Eurena Middleton Verell and Effie India Verell.

Elizan Trooper Allen, born Feb. 11, 1902, one of eight children of Dan and Rachel Trooper. The young man is Al Pierce, born Mar. 25, 1903, son of William and Mildrew Ann Pierce.

Luther and Mattie Nabors and family.

L-R: Leona Carter, Hiram Kimbrough, Eunice Alford and Fred Barnett.

James Richard Kendall and wife, Willie Ann Flemings Kendall. An old newspaper clipping states "Mr. Jim" dug 264 bushels of potatoes in a day and a half from two acres of ground with only nine hands helping him dig and truck them to town.

Annie Mae Guinn Sanderson

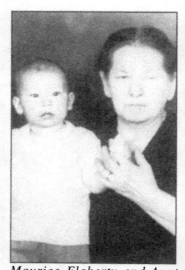

Maurice Flaherty and Aunt Nanny Guinn Flaherty. Maurice was the husband of Thelma Pounds and the father of William Curtis Flaherty.

Cottie Wooldridge Alford, Dessie Moore and Ruby Wooldridge Murfree

Henry Duncan

Lenard Seals and Riley Johnson

Ruby Jernigan Smith, Hazel Jernigan Ellis, ?, Nell Jernigan Butts and Wilma Jernigan Cook, daughters of Jim and Sally Jernigan.

Linnie T. and Lillian Clardy Lacey, 1928

G.D. and Wilma B. Wimberly, picture probably made in 1930.

Lundy Eugene Wilson and friend Colette Martin, probably late 1930s as he was killed in January 1931 when a mule kicked him in the face.

Roy and Lou Welch Alford

Mildred Tate Griffin and Farris Griffin, ca 1930.

Georgia Clark Freeman and Garnette Park Trammell Lancaster, early 1930s, Van Vleet.

Sarah Margaret Pearson Westbrook, mother of Dolly Westbrook Nelson.

James Lee Westbrook and Jewel Palmer (father of Dolly Westbrook Nelson).

James Pounds Tabb (1880-1931), son of Daniel D. and Perline Pounds Tabb, was a lumberman and banker.

Ben Ellis Houser and first wife, Lilly Streeter in the 1930s.

D.R. "Tump" and Lula K. Brown

Thomas Allen House, father of Edgar, James Curtis, Annie Mae, Alonza T., Vera Odell and Clifton H. House.

Maie Weed Wilson holding Lundy Wilson beside Walterene Wilson; Lex Byron Wilson standing. About 1932-33.

The Sullivans, L-R: Minnie, Burdie, Walter and Louise.

L-R: Harold White, Roy Alford, Hasten Alford and Ben Alford.

Adults standing in back, L-R: Dudley Paden, Lula Paden, Ollie A. Davis, Burks Davis holding son, Buck. Children L-R: Raymond Waldrop, Ethel Waldrop Simpson, James Waldrop and Frances V. Davis Priest.

Herbert and Audie Melton Franklin

Jackson (Jack) Weaver and his half sister, Jennie Weaver Melton.

Claude, Audie and Lelon Melton in 1933

Pearl and Emerson Everett with daughters Eva Jean and Evelyn.

L-R: Kenneth D. Barnett and parents, Milton and Lucille Barnett.

John L. Criddle and wife Rena Hatley. Clayton Criddle in background, 1933.

Wallace Moore, Burtram Moore, Thad and Rayburn Sanderson, Betty June Nichols

L- R: Homer Whitt, Jake Criddle, Marvin Gann and Noah Hardin

Emmie Barnett and children.

Left: Josie Melton, early 1930s.

Right: Chester Hollie Harrington (1879-1960) and Biddie Jane Dendy (1881-1965) with their grandson. They were the parents of ten children, Rex, Dan, Hollie, Joise Mae, Travis, Lorette, Weldon, Durell, Ray and Doris.

Bud, Lois, Johnie, Harley and Lorette Langley, Thorn, MS about 1933.

Katie Cox Wilson and Daniel Foster Wilson.

John Marion Evans and Martha (Margaret) Susan (Sammie) Martin Evans

Imogene (Jean) Higginbotham Carter and Eloise Higginbotham

Bro. Jep E. Rogers and Mamie Martin Rogers in the fall of 1934, after their marriage in June.

Noah Lemuel and Iva Merideth Winter with children James Travis and Norine Merideth Winter Turman. Picture made in 1934 of this couple who owned, operated and maintained the telephone exchange in Houlka.

L-R: Edgar, Odell, Tom, Clifton and Aubrey House.

SEVEN GENERATIONS OF THE DUNKLIN SULLIVAN FAMILY

Jarrett Jarvis, son of Jill Wood Jarvis and Don Jarvis.

Jill Wood Jarvis, daughter of Maie Counce Wood and Don Wood.

Lula Maie Counce Wood, daughter of Nola and J.B. Counce.

Nola Cook Counce and J.B. Counce, parents of Maie Counce Wood.

Nannie Sullivan Cook, daughter of Orpha Dye Sullivan and Dunklin M. "Duncan" Sullivan; mother of Nola Cook Counce.

Orpha Dye Sullivan, wife of Dunklin M. "Duncan" Sullivan.

Dunklin M. "Duncan" Sullivan, father of Nannie Cook.

Dunklin Sullivan, 1822-1906, grandfather of Nannie Sullivan Cook.

35

Marion Duke Park (left) and Etoyle Park at Van Vleet School in 1935.

Delia Smith Turman, wife of Aaron Turman and half sister to Mabel Smith Sanderson Davis. Mother of Richard, Allie, Morris, Tabitha, Oral and Francis.

Front row L-R: Lee Davis (1866-1942), his father Reuben Davis (1844-1937). Back row: Mavarlene and baby Ann, with her father, Clarence Davis, Lee's son.

Charlie Anderson and sons, L-R Charles, Bob and Jim, about 1935.

Dr. J.R. Priest, Sr. with granddaughter, Jo Ellen Priest. Born in 1876 in the Redlands District, he was the son of John Pinkney and Teresa Duke Priest. He practiced medicine in Reid, Van Vleet and in Houston from 1921-42. He and his wife, Lorena McIntosh Priest had two sons, Dr. J.R. Priest, Jr. and Mack Priest.

Robert Clifton Kendall, son of James Richard and Willie Ann Flemings Kendall.

Gradion Smith Welch and Roy Alford

Euckley and Minnie Sullivan

William Patterson Doss (left) and Bud Tedder.

Arnold Simpson and Mack Priest

Frances Virginia Davis Priest and Mack Priest; photo made about 1934-35.

Lex Byron Wilson holding Byron Lamar Wilson, 1936.

Curt and Estelle Law, about 1936, Houlka, MS.

Sam and Inez Schwalenburg

William A. Neal (1861-1938)

Joe Forrester, Mantee

Garnette Park Trammell and Rufus Lee Trammell, Van Vleet, 1936.

Avery (Buddy) Pounds and Addie Ellison.

Andrew J. and Pearl O'Barr Weed with grandchildren, Walterene and Lundy Wilson, 1936.

Garnette Park, Tommy Park and Ruby Park; Van Vleet, 1936.

Ludie Mae S. Wimberly, William B. Wimberly and their daughter Mary W. Richards.

Russell L. Kendall with wife Annie Lee Gregory Kendall, daughter Diedra Lynn Kendall and son, Robert Oren Kendall, Pyland, MS.

Leman, Flavius, Hasten and Jewel Alford.

Gus and Lois Vaughn with W.L. Hill.

Delia Carter Smith, Veston Smith and baby Margie Smith Murray.

Eula Bell, Delanie and Ray Hobson, children of Bedford and Laura Buggs Hobson.

Mary Florence Guest Ward, April 1937

The children of John Morgan Davis, Sr. and Virgie Odell Neal. Back row, L-R: John Morgan, Jr., Lemuel Porter, Crawford Gilliam, Malvern Ishmael and Doxie Maddox. Front L-R: Robert Edward (R.E.), Jodie Neal, Mable Benton and Mollie Artie.

Circa 1938-Claude and Rena Mae Moore Johnson with son Bobby and daughter Lucille. Ezekiel T. Moore's blacksmith shop in the background.

Some of the children of Wm. Neal and second wife, Candies Nabors. L-R, back row: Charlie Milton Neal, Lizze Zulene Neal Lyles, Emma Geneva Neal Goza and Wm. Malcolm Neal. Front row, L-R is Candies Neal and Mala Elizabeth Neal Davis.

Some of the children of William and Minnie Davenport Neal: L-R; Haston H. Neal, Mollie Neal Smith, Jadie Neal Thomas, Cliff Neal, George Neal and Baron Neal.

Dendy family reunion, year unknown.

Gene and Margie Smith Murray, 1938.

Evans Lee Gann with daughter Inez (Sissy) Gann Dobbs and granddaughter, Donna Dobbs (Weaver).

Standing: Lynette House Gann (left) and her mother, Gladys Wilson House. Seated is Gladys' mother, Rachel Louise Waldrop Wilson holding Dorothy Ann Gann Wilson daughter of Lynette and Durell Gann. Picture made 1938.

Brothers Claud and Wilton Johnson with their sister, Carrie J. Alford.

Esterline White Earnest, mother of E. J. Earnest, Jr. in the 1930s.

Mollie Johnson, mother of Lela Ann Johnson Earnest, wife of Mose Johnson.

Edward Auston "Son" Martin in the late 1930s.

Ed and Blanche Eaves Lloyd, 1939

Dewey Hobson (Hob) Anderson, between 1930-1940.

Myra and James Hancock

Lillian and James Gann

Lucille Kendall (Betts)

40

LEON MARTIN

Leon Martin is pictured here as a youth, a soldier and a member of his extended Martin family.

He is also shown as a businessman when he purchased the old Dodge-Plymouth dealership from Bert Scarbrough in 1965.

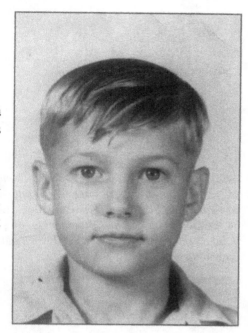

Willie Ann Flemings Kendall, widow of James Richard (Jim Dick) Kendall is flanked by her son and daughter-in-law, Robert Clifton Kendall and Lille Mae Hawkins Kendall. Great grandson Robert O. Kendall looks over her shoulder; great-grandson Ronnie Dale Kendall is in her lap; Bill Kendall, Lynn Kendall and Randy Kendall are on the grass.

Mrs. Edith McCullough of Houlka and her children. Front L-R Patsy (Lusty), Peg (Jade) and Ann (Ellis). Back L-R Joline (Little) Charlotte (McQuary), Mary Alice (Harris), Edith Chrestman McCullough, Deward and Bill.

Jimmy Earnest in front, back l-r is Harold, Tony, Virgie and Austin Earnest.

Ezekiel Thomas Moore (1885-1941) and wife Sevella Higginbotham (1893-1977), parents of Rena Mae, Robert George, Ruby M., Thomas E., Bufford E., Grover E., Virginia M., James E., John A. and Sarah Moore.

Frank Pilgreen, father of Alice Pilgreen Corley, about 1940.

The five daughters of Foster Wilson and Modera Verell. L-R Mary Catherine, Florence Ireda, Meda May, Lessie Margaret and Lesbie Ardice, probably at a "Third Sunday in April" at Enon.

Daisy Mathis Culpepper, daughter of Sam and Anna Culpepper.

Sarah Ann Todd Butler, grandmother of Roy Edward Hill.

Emma Weaver Smith holding son, Tommy; husband Howard Smith and daughter Shirley in front of Flaherty's Store, 1940.

Front L-R: Byron Lamar Wilson, Jack Douglas Wilson and Ruth Wilson Kendall. Back L-R: Walterene (Wally) Wilson Engle, Lex Byron Wilson, Sydney Henderson Wilson and Thomas Lundy Wilson.

The children of Buddy and Alice Hill. Back L-R Betty Jo, Bernice, Joyce. Bottom L-R: Billie, W. L. and Sissy.

James Walter Funderburg and Annie Laura Kirkpatrick Funderburg, 1940s.

L-R: Earline Earnest, Linda White Earnest, Earvin Joseph Earnest, Jr., Dorothy Dean Earnest, Charles E. Earnest and Earvin J. Earnest, Sr. in 1940.

Veston and Delia Smith family in the 1940s.

Left: Willie Eliza Holliday Alexander and Walter Alexander, parents of Jim and DeWitt Alexander, Ollie A. Davis, Ruby A. Moyse, and Ethel A. Jones.

Right: Dr. Deran Hansell began his practice in Egypt in 1910; moving his practice to Okolona in 1919 where hospital rooms were in the old opera hall. After the Tupelo tornado in 1936, he flew some of the victims to Okolona where they were treated without charge.

Jimmy and Bob Anderson of Okolona, about 1940.

Daniel Foster Wilson and Katie Cox Wilson

Sons of Daniel Foster Wilson and Katie Cox Wilson. L-R: Fred Wilson, Joe Wilson, Bob and Turner Wilson.

John Wesley Hill (9/4/1857-10/2/1954) and Ada Craig Hill (12/5/1856-12/8/1943). Picture made about 1940.

Children L-R are Darrell, Dan and Charlene Griffin. Baby is David Roberts. Adults are L-R Lesbie Wilson Griffin and J. D.; Paul Rainey Chenault and Catherine; Ireda Wilson Peacock; Lex Byron Wilson with hands on Charlene; Lessie and Dave Roberts and Foster Wilson. Made at "Granny" Verell's birthday, probably 1941.

Waco and Effie Johnson Reeves with their son, Winston Reeves.

L-R, James Duke, Marion Duke Park, parents Lorena Ashley Duke and Tom A. Duke, Sr., Pauline Duke Smith. Made in the early 1940s.

L-R Paul Lee Mooneyham, son-in-law Arnold Berryhill, Mooney Mooneyham, Hart Mooneyham, Emma Schwalenburg Mooneyham, Bonnie Mooneyham Houser and Gelaine Mooneyham.

Chester Weldon Harrington (1916-1981), his wife Frances Corrinne Weaver (1914-) daughters Linda Faye and Jo Carolyn. Picture made in the early 1940s.

Kathleen Mahan Gore and Tap Laverne Gore shortly after their marriage, about 1945.

L-R: Jim R. Jernigan, Ara Jernigan Tutor and Baxter Jernigan, 1945.

Lou Welch Alford (Mrs. Roy) and Lois Flanagan Welch (Mrs. Gradion Smith Welch)

Jimmie O. Martin's School picture, 1945-46

T.J. and Florence Colburn

Mrs. T.A. Duke, Sr. and grandchildren Jeannette Park (Stevens) and James William Duke, 1945.

Joseph Franklin (Jack) Beaty (1885-1946) with his two grandchildren, Minnie Jo and Lamar Beaty.

Andy Finn bought the Mayfield home in 1921-still stands near Macedonia Methodist Church. Back Row is Andy and Ella Doss Finn's daughter, Minnie Brand, with children Virginia (Pumphrey), Effie Mae (Smith) Hob and Joyce (Porter). Photo circa 1946.

Cortus and Ruby Weaver, about 1946.

Catherine Alexander Simpson and husband, Arnold Simpson.

Laverne and Woodrow Cook, 1947.

Samuel Marion (Manie) Hall, well known business man in Houston, 1947.

Oscar Cooper Neal, Sr. (1878-1949) and wife Sarah Ellen Turman (1880-1950).

Lola Rhodes holding Edwin Hancock.

TRENOR-BROWN FAMILY

The Alex Trenor family, early 1920s, in front of their house near Macedonia. The car is one of the earliest in the county. From left: children Odie, Mamie Lee, Jim; parents James Alexander "Alex" and Mary Etta.

Right: Frank and Maggie Brown, parents of Lizzie Kate Brown Trenor.

Odie Trenor, 1958, at his desk in the Mississippi State Legislature. He represented Chickasaw County for 12 years.

Lizzie Kate Brown Trenor, 1974

The Odie Trenor family at their 50th anniversary party, December 1970. Seated: Lizzie Kate and Odie Trenor. Standing: their children Ewilda (Mrs. James) Fancher, Charles Odie Trenor, Jr. (married Elaine Seemen) and Mary Lee (Mrs. Curtis) Askew.

Five generations: Thomas Randall Kendall held by his great-great-grandmother, Ellen Spence McCluney. Standing, L to R: Glendora Wilson Kendall, Mary McCluney Wilson, Lora Brantley McCluney and husband, Charles Edward McCluney, 1948.

J. Stanton Stewart and Mary Helon Rackley Stewart at home in Houlka, circa 1948.

L-R Carl Spencer, Randolph (Coon) Franklin and Bill Hensley, after working hours at the mill in Pyland.

Maudie Melton Wooldridge

Ben Ellis Houser (1900-1961) son of George Jackson Houser, with his mother Zula Lela Parker Houser. Picture made about 1948.

Lillian Lacey Lowe with son, Lin and two grandchildren in front of the old Greentree Hotel on N. Jefferson Street in Houston.

Burks Davis, father of Frances Priest and "Buck" Davis.

Lacy Kirkpatrick of Houlka, late 1940s.

William Edward (Luck) Jemison with grandaughters Elizabeth C. and Mary M. Jemison, daughters of John Wilkinson Jemison. Houlka, circa 1948.

Tommy Park and son Wayne, Van Vleet, 1948 or 1949.

Ervin and Kathleen Roebuck Wall

L-R Aubrey House, Bro. D.D. Satterwhite and Edgar House.

Willie Wooldridge, son of Jim Wooldridge and husband of Zula Moore.

Perry and Kissie Higgin-botham; Perry was the son of Joe Edmond and Cordelia Higginbotham.

James P. and Katie Sanderson Tabb at their new home on Pontotoc Street (present home of Jack and Nancy Dendy).

Jessie Lee Earnest and wife Lottie Kilgore Earnest

Mary Ann O'Neal Alford, wife of Flavius "Coach Red" Alford.

George "Bud" Roebuck and Minnie Martin Roebuck

George (Fate) and Jessie Moore Wooldridge

Carrie Mae Johnson Alford and Noah C. Alford

Imogene (Jean) Higginbotham Carter and Henry Higginbotham

Henrietta Byars Shearer, (1874-1949) mother of John B., Sally S. Smith, Edward Shearer and Martha S. Parker; grandmother of Martha S. Smith, James M. (Jimmy) Smith and Virginia S. Thornton.

Hal Tucker Jolly, Sr. and wife, Virginia Ruth Harris. Hal was a stock trader and farmer. He served as Sheriff and Tax Collector of Chickasaw County from 1948 to 1952.

Annie Lee Gregory Kendall and Russell Lee Kendall

Lucian and Lavonia Lloyd, parents of Ed Lloyd; grandparents of Becky Lloyd Duke and Jim Lloyd.

Jessie Benton (Jake) Martin and Sue Jean Martin Black

Mrs. Scottie Bates Tabb, granddaughter of Judge Thomas N. Martin, mother of Wm. Bates Tabb.

Children of Oscar Cooper Neal, Sr. and Sarah Ellen Turman. Back L-R: William Rex (Billy), Herrod Richard, Robert Evans and Leon Curtis. Standing in middle is Grace Lavonia with Sarah Louise, Oscar C., Jr (O.C.) and Susie Mae.

From top to bottom: Gladys Butler Springer, Billy Clyde Hill, Miriam Spruell, Marie Spruell and Roy Edward Hill.

Annie (Melton) Welch, Louise (Wooldridge) Rhodes and Macee (Melton) Welch

Betty and Rad Clark with son, David.

Jeanette Lowry Pumphrey, age 21

J.S. "Old Timer" Earp, Sr. and Jimmy Earp

L-R: Mack Priest, Willie Foster, Garland Stewart, Johnny Gholson and Arnold Simpson.

Mattie Kyle Jemison, wife of John Wilkinson Jemison, Sr.

Barita Gregg Davis, nurse at Houston Hospital and wife of Pompey Davis.

Wilton and Emma Johnson

Myrtle Lee Byars Park and James Eldridge Park, Van Vleet, in the 1950s.

L-R: Jennie Weaver, W.C. Weaver, Angie Armstrong Weaver and J.C. Weaver.

Children L-R: Raymond Wooldridge, Louise and Libby Wooldridge; Back L-R: Ben Alford, Atwell Wooldridge and Cottie Wooldridge Alford at Thorn, Mississippi.

Benjamin Franklin (Ben) and Mattie Lanham Earp

Family reunion at the J.E. Davis and Mable Smith Sanderson Davis home in the 1950s.

THE LANGLEY FAMILY

The Langley family has been in Chickasaw County since 1885, when Eli Von and Camely Searcy Langley moved their family from Tuscaloosa, Alabama, becoming some of the earliest settlers of Thorn Community. Will Langley, their son, was 9-years-old when the family moved, and he remained to rear his family in Thorn.

Will's grandson, Harley Langley, son of Bud and Lois Langley, married Sue Fleming, daughter of Joe Lee and Dede Fleming of Calhoun County. Harley and Sue returned to the Langley family farm in Thorn, in 1974, after living out of the state 20 years. Now, Harley and Sue, their three children and their families all live in Chickasaw County.

Randy and Diane Langley, with their children, Joe and Rachel, live in the Hot Air Community; Kathy and Joe Black, and their children, Daniel and Justin, live in Thorn; Renee and Keith Davis and their son Will, live in Thorn.

The Langley's own and operate Southern Funeral Chapel in Houston.

Harley Langley

Sue Fleming Langley

Joe Lee Fleming, 1995

Sue

Harley and Johnnie Langley, 1934

Randy, Renee and Kathy, 1964

Randy and Kathy, 1958

Renee and Kathy, 1967

Will and Sally Langley

Jerrell, Sue, Joe Lee and Dede

Lois Langley and Eunice Wooldridge, November 2001

Kathy, Sue, Renee, Harley and Randy, 1964

Randy, Kathy and Paula with Renee, Shelia and Rita

Justin, Will, Sue, Harley, Rachel, Daniel, Kathy, Renee, Diane, Joseph, Joe, Keith and Randy, 1996

Rachel, Sue, Harley, Joe, Daniel, Justin and Will, 2000

Left: Bud and Lois Langley

Right: Joe and Dede Fleming, 1950

Maxine Lowry Brown at age 18.

John and Giree Chenault

Valine Dendy Pulaski and husband, Maurice R. Pulaski.

Dr. J. Rice Williams (1894-1953) left general medicine to confine his work to X-Ray diagnosis and "deep therapy" at the Houston Hospital. He first married Nona Hobson; after her death, he married Florence Ford of Houston.

Dr. Richard Garland Hendrick practiced medicine in Okolona for 20 years before his death at age 48.

Claude and Celestine Weaver with children, Jerry and Judy, 1952.

Ca 1950. L-R front: Bessie Sullivan (Thompson), Joe Wesley Sullivan and Mattie Rowena Jolly Sullivan. Standing L-R: Earl, Mary Sullivan (Spencer), Eugene and Rufus Sullivan, Bera Sullivan (Ogg), Charlie, Jonell Sullivan (Hill), Clyde "Guinea" and Wesley Sullivan. This family descends from the pioneer Sullivan family of the Chalk Bluff Community, south of Okolona.

Jim and Mattie McQuary's 13 children in 1952 at the home of M.M. (Roe) McQuary. According to age and from L-R back row: Riley McQuary, Marion Monroe McQuary, Cora Alice (Alto) McQuary Dendy, Pearl McQuary Jennings, Edd McQuary, Jesse McQuary, Jack McQuary. Front row, L-R: Minnie McQuary Nabors, Carnie McQuary Turnage, Hosea McQuary, Rena McQuary Nabors, John McQuary, Lera McQuary Hamilton.

Left: Susan Eurena Middleton Verell, (1865-1958) daughter of Thomas Holland Middleton and Martha Ann Wills; wife of Eugene Milton Verell.

Middle: Clara Houser Martin, George Jackson Houser and Ben Ellis Houser at the graveside of Zula Parker Houser; Arbor Grove Cemetery, 1953.

Right: Susie Law of Houlka with granddaughters Patsy Law (left) and Sue Smith, about 1953.

Left: Phillip Clark "Sambo" Martin (left) and Leon Martin, 1953

Middle: Johnny Ardell Martin and Mamie L. Wheeler Martin, December 1953.

Right: James (Jim) Hugh Tabb (1908-1994) son of James P. and Katherine (Kate) Sanderson Tabb. Like his father, he was prominent in the lumber business, local banking, church and community affairs.

Roy Lee and Dovie Williams with daughters Margie and Doris, 1954.

David W. Allen and wife Frances with children Kaye and Alice.

Left: Joe William Kilgo, Ray Johns and Clayton Corley at Boones' Chapel Methodist Church, Okolona, MS. 1954.

Middle: Tommy Hugh Smith, son of Howard and Emma Smith holding Vickie Rose Huffman Barnett in front of "English" Ford car in 1955.

Right: Durell and Lynette House Gann in the mid 1950s.

Laura and Bedford Hobson, 1955 with 9 of their 11 children. Lula and Ida had died before this picture. Front L-R: Oda, Bedford, Laura, Oscar, and Delanie. Back L-R: Ruth, Eula, Ray, Cassie, Mattie and Florence. Ray was a nurse; Eula a beautician; Florence, Oda and Ruth were teachers.

Jess and Loree Clark Warnick

Dr. H.F. Crumby graduated from the Univ. of TN Medical School in 1913; practiced until 1968.

James Edward Dendy and Myrtie Scarbrough Dendy

Albert Franklin (Buck) Huffman

Vida O'Barr Huffman

L-R-back: Jimmy J. (Jim) Martin, Ethel Griffin, Charles Aaron Martin, David Earl Hill, Louise Martin Hill with Rachel; Jimmie Martin Wages and Charles Wages; Middle row: John Allan Martin, Jerry Mack Martin, Rita Carol Martin with Petie Hill in front.

Couples from left to right: Sue and Ray Boone, Murray (Tater) and Dolly Nabors and Harold and Loyce Turner, 1956 or 1957.

Lottie Rogers Corley and her children, Eddie and Ann with Carolyn in the wagon, 1958.

Bill and Betty Earnest Linley with children Delois Ann and Wanda Gail Linley.

Harold Stevens, wife Jeannette Park Stevens and daughter, Donna, June 1959.

Son Weaver (left) and Travis Harrington

Standing L-R: Wilma (Wid) Scarbrough, Floy S. Landreth, Tom Scarbrough, Darell Scarbrough and Curt Scarbrough. Seated L-R: Myrtie S. Dendy with parents Alice and Preston Scarbrough.

Ruby Jewel Davidson (1915-1974) daughter of Milas Lee and Clara Florence Hadley Davidson, and husband Henry Royce Culpepper, Sr. (1912-1980), son of William Alexandra Culpepper.

L-R Jeffie McGill Chadick, born 1906; Sula McGill David, born 1902.

James William Culpepper, son of William Alexander Culpepper.

J.D. and Lesbie (Wilson) Griffin

Mrs. Jessie Doss Gann with her three children, L-R, Leonard, Durell and Mae Helen Gann Nelson.

Roy P. "Pompey" Davis, Houston's Chief of Police, with son Keith and daughter, Beth, at their home on Park Street, about 1961.

"Miss Daisy" Coyle with great-granddaughters Donna and Karen Dobbs, about 1962.

Miller Clark, Iris Clark Mooneyham, Pat Clark, Eunice Clark Wooldridge, Bob Clark and Lois Clark Langley, children of Franklin Harley Clark and Della Maharrey Clark, about 1963.

Right: Four of the children of Jim and Vicie Wooten. Front L-R: Anna Bell (Criddle) and Lizzie (Mauldin). Back L-R: Susie (O'Barr) and Lula (Whitted). Not in the picture is a brother, Bill Wooten and a sister, Sally (Martin). Circa 1965.

Mrs. Ora Felton Goza (Miss Felton) and husband, Sam Goza.

Everette and Bernice Clark Smith

Sally Ida Free Kilgore holding her birthday cake; she was the wife of Smith Kilgore. Her son William is on the porch.

Blanche and Cliff Chandler, Okolona, MS

Five generations–Mrs. Hill (Leona) Smith with her son Howard, his daughter Shirley, her daughter Vickie and her daughter Deborah Denise Dendy.

Malcolm Wicks Culpepper, son of Henry Royce and Ruby Jewel Davidson Culpepper.

Jadie Neal Thomas

L-R: brothers Jack, Milt, Enix and Felix Barnett.

Gertie and Roy Filgo of Okolona, MS, 1970

Florence and Willie Lee Priest of Okolona, MS, 1970

Candice Nabors Neal, second wife of William A. (W.E.) Neal, 1971.

Howard and Nettie Sue Peden Ray, Van Vleet, March 1978

Alice Pilgreen Corley at her home south of Okolona in the "Shakerag" Community, circa 1983.

Marie Priest Brown with her son, Richard and daughter, Roxanne. Photo made 1985.

Left: Mrs. Burks Davis, age 90; Mrs. Margaret (Maggie) Boring Baine, age 90; and Mrs. Lorena McIntosh Priest, age 93. Picture made 1980.

L-R: Mary Margaret Stewart McKell, Nannette S. Rowan, Syble Nanney Stewart, William Clyde Stewart, Ladye Clyde S. King and William Clyde "Bill" Stewart, Jr., 1990s.

Robert and Bobbie Corley

Howard Huffman (1957-1996) son of Mr. and Mrs. A.J. Huffman and Mrs. Shirley Logan.

Children of George Wes Clark and Elizabeth "Lizzie" Martin, L-R: Florence Stroup, Lillie Sanders, Mary Nolen. Standing L-R James "Virt" Clark, Ira "Pete" Clark and Leroy Clark.

Royce Culpepper, son of Henry Royce and Ruby Jewel Davidson Culpepper.

A.J. and Evelyn Tackett Huffman

Funderburg family reunion, 1993. L-R: Irene Washington, Estelle Law, Julia McCammon, Katie Oxner, Jean Gregory, Ruby Luther and Helen West. Kneeling is sister-in-law Jean Funderburg and sitting is Lula Jean Gregory.

Five generations. Standing is Grandmother Jenise Turman and son Kevin Turman, father. Seated is Johnnie Duncan, great-grandmother, and Lois Langley, great-great-grandmother.

BURT-MCKEE FAMILY

Martha Elizabeth McKee graduated from high school at Batesville in 1937. Her graduating class is pictured at the First Methodist Church where her father delivered the sermon. She left for college in Georgia.

Her mother's illness brought her back to Mississippi where she was teaching when she met James Augustus Burt, Jr. who had left college to go into World War II. They were married at First Presbyterian Church in Houston by the Rev. W.F. Patch. He was finishing up training in time for them to celebrate their first wedding anniversary on February 28, 1943, at the Peabody Skyway in Memphis. He spent most of three years in the Pacific.

FOUR GENERATIONS OF BURT PREP SCHOOL GRADUATES

James Augustus Burt, Sr.
(1882-1956) Pittsboro Academy

James Augustus Burt, Jr.
(1921-1999) Houlka H.S. 1939

James Augustus Burt, III
(born 1947) Jackson Murrah H.S.

James Augustus Burt, IV
(born 1980) Houlka H.S.

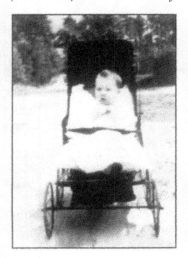

Left: Baby picture of Martha.

Middle: Martha at age 8 with sister Mary Alice, age 4.

Right: Jimmy (James A. Jr.), age 8

Burt-McKee Family

Jimmy's family were good to visit Martha while she lived at the home of her father and he was overseas. His favorite neice, Bobbyie Jean Long, often spent the night so she could attend school events. Mother Burt, Brother Tyron (until he left for the Army) and sister-in-law Helen came with her.

Shown are classmates' children: the Holladays, Burts, Youngs, Normans and Cains (Laverne Harwood)

Marriage involved four classmates to each other: Roncyl and Emma Sue Hobson with their children, Ronnie, Sue, William and Marcia; Leland Brown Norman and Louise Bullard with Martha Carol and Leland, Jr. and Mimi shown in other photo on mother's lap.

The Burts moved to Jackson where both Betty and Jim graduated from Murrah High. Betty was an honor grad of Millsaps College and met her future husband in the psychology classroom. She married Wm. A. Bolick at U. of KY after graduate school.

Martha Elizabeth was born as the war began, James III after Jimmy came home. We lived in Clarksdale and had few chances to see Class of 1939 associates of Jimmy. 1953 was an exception when some of them gathered for a picnic. Here are Jimmy, Martha, Betty and Jim at Davis Lake.

Baby Mimi Norman was too little to pose for the group. Only a few months old she was photographed on her mother's lap.

Jim graduated from Wood College and received a business degree from Mississippi State University.

The Bolicks moved to Wisconsin. Betty joined a tour on Russian Air Line in the days when they were still searching hotel luggage. Betty and fellow tour member shown in Russia.

BURT-MCKEE FAMILY

Martha McKee Burt placed the histories and pictures of her husband's Chickasaw ancestor families in the Chickasaw County History, Vols. 1 and 2. She researched other families for the society. Now that she has been living here for 19 years, she feels she can now qualify as a Chickasaw Countian and include some history of her families in the county publication.

Maternal grandparents: Martha Elizabeth Hill and husband Josiah Fleming Duncan. Martha E. was born 1856 at Hazel, KY. She died in 1918 just after this picture was made in Oklahoma where they moved to be near two sons. Josiah Fleming was born at Hartsville, TN, in 1848, son of Dr. Fleming Willis Duncan and Phoebe Hatcher Marshall.

Phoebe Hatcher Marshall (1829-1915) was born Goose Creek, Sumner County, TN, where several of her families pioneered from Virginia. We have good Colonial records.

Martha Elizabeth Duncan, tintype at age 16; eldest child of Josiah and Martha.

Tomasia Glen Duncan (1892-1949), youngest daughter of Josiah and Martha, in her McFerrin College graduation dress all hand drawn and sewn by older sister Martha Elizabeth.

Tomasia Duncan married Hugh Robert McKee as his second wife. They are Martha McKee Burt's parents. Picture was made 1941 with a grandson, John Robert McLeod, son of Hugh's eldest daughter, Ersula.

Hugh Robert McKee (1882-1983) left a good business and became a Methodist minister in 1912. He preached at First Methodist on his 100th birthday on area television and christened Martha and Jimmy Burt's first grandchild, James Augustus IV.

Wm. Robert McKee III, son of Hugh Kelsey and Elizabeth Campbell McKee (1856-1923) was married to Nancy Ann Drake. These parents gave son, Hugh Robert, clerical heritage: two Drake Church of England vicars before 1650 and the first Presbyterian minister in North Carolina.

Hugh Robert McKee with his children on his 91st birthday in Jackson at Martha's home. Martha seated on floor and Mary Alice are Tomasia's children; the others, Mary Edwina, Frances Lorena, Samuel Melvin, Oscar Clade and Laura Ersuls are the children of Lela Pernicia Vick who died in the 1918 influenza epidemic.

BURT-McKEE FAMILY

Left: Wm. T. and Martha E. Duncan Johnson whom Martha Burt knew as "Popsy and Little Mother." They traveled many a mile in this old Tin Lizzie.

Right: Clarence (nee Franks) Johnson, adopted son of Popsy and Little Mother from a Tennessee River Boat Pilot who had lost his wife. With degrees in history, Clarence made a name with the National Park Service, helping to develop Chalamette and Atlanta and participating in many of those great radio dramas of the 1930s and 1940s. Just behind him is Tomasia and two college friends.

The Duncan sisters: Ethel (Hay), Ruby (Neisler), Martha E. (Johnson), Tomasia (McKee) 8 years old, Lillie Louise (LeCornu) sitting for the picture in Fulton, KY.

Tomasia Glen Duncan following Vanderbilt-Peabody Graduate School.

Left: Another picnic, circa 1916.

Right: Along the Cumberland River near Nashville in 1917. Tomasia in dark dress with Clarence, Little Mother and Popsy.

BURT-MCKEE FAMILY

Jimmy posed with PBY like the one he crewed in the Pacific, 1943-45.

Martha on Mother's Day 1976 ready to take off with son Jim as his first passenger.

Betty on a visit from Wisconsin to Jackson with companion Winston Churchill II.

Betty Burt Bolick honoree at awards dinner with spokesperson June Allyson who advertised Betty's first patented product for Kimberly-Clark.

Jim, Rebel and the beloved mustang.

Jim and wife Jane leave Louisville, KY, hospital with James Augustus IV.

Second grader Jennifer

Right: Jennifer Jane Burt, Pontotoc High Class of 2002.

Jimmy with his mother, Lillie Permelia Brown Burt (1886-1979) on her last birthday.

CHILDREN OF LONG AGO

Celeste Byars Clark, Van Vleet, late 1800s.

Cortus Weaver, son of Tom Henry and Angie Armstrong Weaver.

George Wesley Blissard, 1874-1959

Frank Houser

Blanche Edens (Chandler) made in early 1900's, Okolona, MS.

Catherine Shell Davis, about 1905

Robert Preston Williams, 1906-1984

Thomas M. Gore, born 1906

Left: Mae Lorene Ford Johnson, mother of Ella McCullough.

Middle: Children of John Morgan Davis, Sr. and Virgie O'Dell Neal, L-R: Jodie Neal, b. 1905; Mabel Benton, b. 1908; and Ida R.E., b. 1903.

Right: Lex Byron Wilson and Eugene Graydon Verell, circa 1909-10.

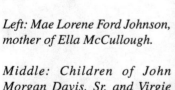

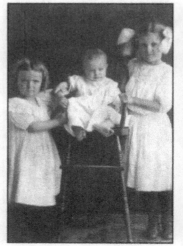

Joseph Elias Weaver, seated, and his brother Frank.

Josie Melton, about age three.

Jacob Hardin on his way to "Sunbeams."

Tommy Park and Ruby Park Brock in 1912.

James K. Vardaman (Boozie) Sanderson holding his half-brother, Edward Davis.

Frances Virginia Davis Priest and her brother, Kenneth "Buck" Davis.

L-R: Eldridge Smith, Willie Coy Smith and Howard Hugh Smith, sons of Hill and Leona Smith.

Children of George W. and Laura Wheeler Carter: Standing is Lester Carter; Left to R-Cornelia Carter Pumphrey and Delia Carter Smith.

Leo and Cleo Weed, twin children of A.J. and Pearl O'Barr Weed on "Old Dock."

The three oldest children of Daniel Foster Wilson and Modera Verell - Lesbie, (1909-1966); baby is Lundy Eugene (1912-1931) and Lex Byron Wilson (1906-1948). Picture ca 1913.

Rena Mae Moore, born 1912, oldest child of Ezekiel T. and Sevella H. Moore.

Tommy Park, Van Vleet, about 1915-16

Jim Hugh Tabb and his sister, Rosalynd. Picture made about 1915.

Jodie Davis Gormerly, born 1905, and now a resident of Floy Dyer Manor in Houston.

W.A. Skelton, Jr. and "Ole Minnie," 1915

Garnette Park Trammell Lancaster, Van Vleet, 1917

Grace Wilson Beaty Eaton, born 6-17-1914; mother of Lamar Beaty and Minnie Jo Hill.

W. Clyde Stewart, Sr., about 10 years old; Houlka, MS. ca 1918.

Max Duke and Marion Duke Park, early 1920s.

Myrtie Scarbrough Dendy

Joseph Kimball Beaty (1911-1952) and his mule, Maude.

Garnette Park and her brother Tommy Park, 1922.

Sydney Ethel Henderson (Wilson) in 1924 at the age of 17.

Catherine Shell Davis at about 12 years of age.

Leona Carter Kimbrough, 1910-1997

Opal Dendy Gore

The children of Nannie Sullivan and Carl Cook - Tura, Nola, Eugene and Tennyson.

Nola Cook, daughter of Nannie Sullivan and Carl Cook; Ethel Sullivan, daughter of Murdock "Dock" Sullivan.

Bobby and Anne Dexter Pearson, late 1929, in Houston.

Right: Annie Mae Talley Anderson with her sons, L-R Charles, Bob and Jim, circa 1933.

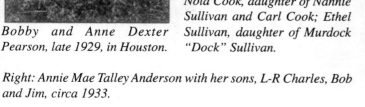

Henry Higginbotham, Pyland, Mississippi

Opal Dendy Gore (left) and Laurice Dendy Terry

Jimmy Smith and sisters Virginia Smith Thornton and Martha Smith Smith about 1936.

Betty Joan Gordon, 1936 or 1937

L.C. Duncan

L-R: Joan Lowry, Elizabeth Lowry and Annie Ray House in front of Doss Lowry home.

James Jasper Melton, son of Granville and Coley M. Melton, 2 years old in 1937.

Ed Lloyd seated on his hog with brother, Sam Lloyd.

Atwell Wooldridge and Floyd White

Seated, L to R: Walterene Wilson, Patsy Griffin, Cleo and Leo Weed. Standing, L to R: James Weed holding Lundy Wilson, Josie Weed.

Sissy Gann Dobbs and her dog, December 1937.

Joyce Kimbrough Smith at the old Allen Wooldridge store which later became the M.J. Walter's Grocery Store, Thorn, MS

Walterene Wilson, 1939-40

Mary Catherine Wilson, Woodland School; her shirt is autographed with friends' names. 1939-40

Back row L-R: Joann Mixon, Don Harrington, Alex Springer and Mackie Weaver. Front is Dot Gann Wilson, May Helen Gann Nelson, Tommy Harrington obscured by Barbara Weaver Fleming, G.W. Harrington and Harry Dendy.

L-R: Mackie and Robert Weaver

Geneva Neal Goza

Naomie and Opal Kimbrough

Byron Lamar Wilson with his dog, Sue, 1940

Ronnie Patch and Beverly Davis at a Tom Thumb wedding.

Betty Mack Priest Brown

Front, L-R: Mava Melton and Libby Wooldridge. Back row, L-R: Gerald Cook, Ruth Ann Melton, Louise Wooldridge, Ray Wooldridge and Marie Melton.

Robert Oren Kendall

Dale Mooneyham

Jeannnette Park (Stevens), 1941

Delia Ann and Willie Edd Murray in the 1940s.

74

L-R: Lynette Hardin, Sue Baird, Sissy Gann, Bobby Earl Matthews, Tommy Baird and Joan Gann.

Left to right in a "Radio Flyer" at Pyland, MS: Daphne Franklin, Lynn Kendall and Lynette Franklin.

Gene and Glyn Smith, twin grandchildren of twin, Lula Hill Robertson.

James S. (Jimmy) Gore and James Robert Ford

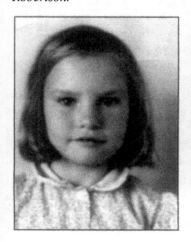

Left: Sally Earnest Kendall, 1940-41

Middle: Mae Helen Gann Nelson, 1941-42

Right: Jack Wilson in front of his big brothers, Byron Lamar on the left and Thomas Lundy Wilson on the right, summer 1942.

The "Gore" boys in 1942. L-R: Jimmy, Edward and Sammy in the front yard of Mr. "Bud" Saxon's rental house.

James M. (Jimmy) Hood, Jr. and Hulet Hobson at Dr. J.M. Hood's office in Houlka.

Byron Lamar Wilson, 1943

Left: Rena Criddle with her children, Joe E. and Eva Ann, about 1944.

Right: Robert Oren (Bob-O) Kendall stands in the old water fountain at the Pyland School. On the bicycle is his uncle, Robert Hawkins Kendall. The Navy "flat hat" and the white cap probably belonged to John Clifton, uncle and brother, who was in the Navy.

Ann Brand, her brother Woodrow, Jr., holding their sister, Nancy in 1944.

Byron Lamar Wilson, left; center from back to front: Walterene, Jack and Ruth Wilson; right: Lundy Wilson.

Stafford and Billy Clyde Woodruff near the old Dayton Woodruff Store.

Dorothy Ann Gann (Wilson), 1944-45 school year

Thomas Lundy Wilson, 1945-46

Flavius "Red" Alford, 1945-46

Jack Douglas Wilson, 1945-46

Robert Hawkins "Hawk" Kendall, 1946-47

Lois Earnest (Kendall), 1946-47

Thomas Hollie Kendall, 1946-47

William Dreifus Kendall, 1946-47

It's 1946 and Penney Cox (Nichols) and her brother Gerry Cox ride "Billy" while their great-grandfather, A.C. Baird stands by. A.C. was the grandfather of Willie Baird Cox and father of Osma E. Baird.

L-R: Mary Alice Patch (McAlister); Martha Ann Patch (Fox) and Betty Patch (Tonges).

The grandchildren of J.W. and Elvia Guyton Hatley, winter of 1947-48. (All L-R.) Front: Helen Louise and Mary Elizabeth Hatley, Mary Jane Criddle. Second row: Betty Sue Hatley and Eva Ann Criddle. Third row: Joe Criddle and Nova Lou Hatley.

Pyland, MS - some in suits and some in rubber boots - date and occasion unknown L-R: Sambo Bevils, Shorty Thomas, Billy Gene Sykes, Joe Wiley Bevils, Charles Bevils, Hawkins Kendall, Ed Sykes with arms around Bobby Joe Sykes.

Joyce Gann Naron, 1948-49

Tom Thumb Wedding, 1948 or 49. L-R: Lynne McKnight, Judye Kyle, Betty Scott, Mary Ann Scott, Nancy Tabb, Robbie Lee Horn, Mary Grace Furr, Jeannie Eastridge, Martha Carole Norman, Gayle Harris, Linda Farr, Betty Patch, Beth Bray and Wade Peeples.

Cathleen and Charleen Duncan, about 1950.

Marie Priest Brown

Alice (left) and Kaye Allen, children of David and Frances.

James David Alford and Curtis Paul Alford with a chain-driven tricycle, 1953.

Betty Earnest (Linley), 1952-53

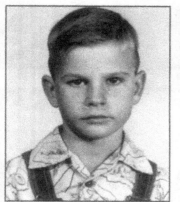

Harold Earnest

Jimmy Earnest

Virgie Earnest

Tom Thumb Wedding presented by the Culture Club of Houston for the benefit of the children's section of the local library. Front L-R: Sarah Ann Miller, Ann Worden, Lynette Hardin and Mary Alice Patch and Ann Brand. Others include Yvonne Carty, Louise McIntosh, Dorothy Ann and Joyce Gann, Jimmy and Edward Gore.

Otis Mooneyham

Elizabeth Ann Corley (Cook) age 3 and James Edward, "Eddie" Corley, age 4 in the Chalk Bluff Community south of Okolona, 1957.

Kevin, Keith, Beth and Lynn Davis in front of their father, Roy P. "Pompey" Davis' police car, about 1965.

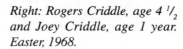

Left: Barry K. Clark, (1962-1972) son of Rad and Betty Clark.

Right: Rogers Criddle, age 4 ¹/₂ and Joey Criddle, age 1 year. Easter, 1968.

GLIMPSES FROM THE PAST

Left: Joel Pinson (1786-1852). In 1836, Pinson donated 80 acres for the town of Houston, named for his good friend, Sam Houston.

Right: George Jackson Houser's Sawmill, ca 1910/11 in the Arbor Grove Community, was later moved to Bentley, MS, after a storm destroyed much of the timber. Bethlehem Church was built from salvaged lumber and stands today in the Bentley Community of Calhoun Co.

Andrew Jackson Ford in front of Sparks' Grocery, Montpelier, MS.

A good example of the "Dogtrot" style of homes. Standing in front of their home is John Luke Davis and third wife, Mattie Martin. House was disassembled, moved and reassembled at the museum at Ballard Park, Tupelo, MS.

Dr. J.R. Priest, Sr. on his horse Dan, ready to visit another patient. Photo made about 1917.

Family and friends gather to help Alex Trenor clear land in the Macedonia area, about 1918.

A postcard sent to Katie Sanderson Tabb, date unknown. The message reads: "Dear Kati, Glad to hear that you are on foot again-Thought of you Tuesday 7th and wished so much that I could spend the day with you. Mr. C. says he wants me to bring Jim Hugh back with me when I go home. This picture was made at a club meeting but it was a bad day and all the members were not there. We had played Rook. They made the tall ones sit - so of course I "sat." Write me. Ida (Sanderson Cheatham)"

East side of the Square in Houston, year unknown.

North side of the Square in Houston, year unknown.

Chickasaw County's Courthouse was built in 1908 and early 1909. W.J. McGee was the builder, R.H. Hunt the architect. W.T. Johnson was president of the Board of Supervisors, George Bean was sheriff. The Building Commission included D.D. Tabb, A.M. Harley and I.V. Abernethy. Seen here, the building is complete, but dirt surrounds it.

Looking North from the "College" in Houston, date unknown.

Looking east toward the Court Square from Hwy 8 West (mostly unpaved) in Houston.

A busy sawmill located in Schooner Valley, typical of the many mills operating in the early 20th century.

View of Main Street, Okolona, MS, date unknown.

Looking down on the south side of the court square in Houston. Date and occasion unknown.

Right: Dredging Mud Creek in the 1920s.

Looking east at the intersection of Main and Gatlin street in Okolona, date unknown. Confederate Memorial monument in foreground still stands.

Looking east on Hwy. 8 at the railroad tracks toward the Court Square of Houston.

Looking south on N. Jackson Street at about the intersection of Hamilton Street. What is now Pearson's Drug Store is on left, old Houston Hotel can be seen in the rear, left side. Present site of Treasure Trove and Telecap on right side of picture.

Annie Ruth Harris Harrington, about 1920, as a student nurse in one of the early nursing classes of Dr. Van Philpot, Sr. From Meridian, she rode the train to Houston, where she met and married Lawrence Harrington who drove the bus-taxi from the train.

Rena Mae Moore in the 1920s.

Robert A. Stewart in the 1920s. A rural mail carrier from June 1920 to December 1965. He carried mail on horseback, two wheel cart, buggy, mail wagon, Model T Ford and closed his career with a Ford Fairlaine 500.

Dr. W.C. Walker (left) and Dr. J.M. Hood at Houlka, Mississippi about 1923.

L-R: Mose White, Bennie Williams, Joe Doss and George Higginbotham.

Leroy "Red" King and road grader, date unknown.

While obviously not approved by OSHA, this dredge boat was typical of those used to excavate creeks, channels and rivers in our area. This picture was made in 1923. Mr. A.H. (Hubert) Houston of Houlka, MS was a fireman. The living quarters on the back were where he and his wife lived when they first married. Overall dimensions were 20 x 60. A 1/2 cubic yard bucket on a boom sawed from white oak timbers, steel reinforced, removed the muck and mud.

"Courtin Days, 1924," Grace Taylor Scott and Walter E. (Bubba) Scott, Jr..

North Jackson Street, Houston, MS, about 1924. First house on left is the Hill house, later known as W.E. Scott residence, just beyond it is the Isaac Paulk home. On the right is the Harley Hill home and just beyond it is the Jamison home.

Annie Mae Talley Anderson of Okolona, about 1925.

Eunice Clark Wooldridge as a young girl; she died in 2002 at age 103.

A.J. Harrington, Jr. and his cousin Lawrence Harrington with a string of quail, about 1927.

The turning lathe at the Chickasaw Handle Company of Houston, established in 1946 by James McCullough, Thurman Lowe, Elbert Hensley and Frederick Swan.

Lex Byron Wilson and Alma Maie Weed Wilson; photo made between 1928 and 1933.

Opal Dendy Gore

Mae Henry with ax and hoe and Angela Wilson, in front of the old log home of D.C. (Lump) Chenault.

Looking west at Hwy. 8 in Houston. The old First Baptist Church building is on the left.

The crew that worked the John Harris steam engine sawmill, date unknown.

Looking west on Hwy. 8 from railroad in Houston. Toomer Lumber Co. on right.

Jessie Benton (Jake) Martin and Virginia Duncan Martin

At Thorn, Mississippi, between 1930-35. Front row, L-R: Claude Alford, Lin Alford, John Henry Wooldridge, Joe Doss and ?. Back row, L-R: Hosie Griffin, ? and Hasten Alford.

The old farmhouse of Bedford and Laura Hobson with grandchildren riding horses

Walton Blissard and Homie Anderson in their courting days.

J.L. Kendall home when owned by Ivorys, about 1935. Store window says "Robert Ivory - Plumbing, Heating and Electric."

Mobile and Ohio Railroad Depot in Okolona. Destroyed by fire in 1968.

Houston Hotel (demolished in the 1950s) is the backdrop for a parade. Year unknown, possibly 1936. Probably a church parade as the Christian Flag flies by the US flag.

After killing hogs, December 10, 1937; E.L Gann, ?, J. Lowe Ford

Thomas E. Moore, son of Ezekiel and Sevella Moore, delivering library books to Thorn residents in the 1930s.

Nettie Sue Peden and Grace Wilson both graduated in 1933 and had a double wedding in 1934. Nettie Sue married Howard Ray and Grace married Kimball Beaty.

"Pa" Jack Sykes on left and Everett Franklin with the results of a grappling trip for catfish in the Pyland bottom.

Houston's first theatre, owned by Arthur and Ruth Rush, pictured here with Jack Buckingham and Waldo Kyle at left. John and Mable Davis' Cafe is seen on the right and the Sugarbowl Cafe on the left. Note sign "Western Electric Sound System."

Fannie M. Lowry about to receive the first "Air Mail" to be delivered in Houston in 1939.

Sarah Frances Griffin Alford at the back porch water bucket.

Counter of the old Houston Hotel, at the SE corner of Hwys. 8 and 15 in Houston. Note radio speaker above signs. Advertisements are for R.C. Pearson's Style Shop, D.M. Hearne's Dry Goods, Crump's Cleaners, Coca Cola, and Atwater Kent Radios, and Justice Co.

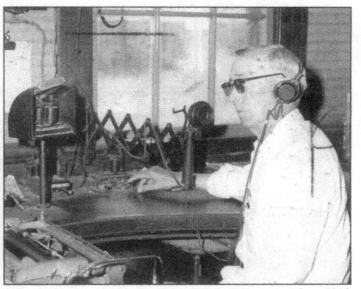

Dr. Samuel Kirkham Gore in his office in Houston, Mississippi.

J. Grady Graves was depot agent at Houlka, Mississippi from 1918 to 1942.

Dr. Van Philpot, Sr., Chief of Staff of Houston Hospital.

A view of the lobby of the old Houston Hospital.

Main Street in Okolona in the early 1940s.

E.J. Earnest, Jr. and brother Charles are surrounded by section hands near the site of the old OH & CC (Okolona, Houston and Calhoun City) railroad depot near the intersection of Pittsboro and Pontotoc Streets in Houston.

Tommy Lee Parker by the old Houston Hospital, 1942. He began working there in 1924 at the age of 17 and worked in various capacities there for 61 years.

The old Thorn Post Office and Store with Lorena Lovelace and Ova "Mama Ovie" White.

Clyde and Syble Stewart, circa 1944.

Roy and Lucille Betts in front of their Flight 21 Restaurant. The menu offers Bar-B-Que for 30¢; hamburger with cheese for 25¢.

Guards at Gulf Ordnance Plant, Prairie, Mississippi, during World War II. Many Chickasaw Countians worked here, making ammunition. John L. Criddle of Houston is nearest camera of the three in line between road and flagpole. Martha Gilliam Clark of Houston is the tallest of the six ladies.

Lion Service Station at the corner of Madison and Jefferson, operated by W.L. Pumphrey. The boy is William Arnold Sisk; 1945.

The John Paden blacksmith shop in Houlka. L-R: James Paden, John Paden and Mack Paden.

Doss and Fannie Lowry with blue ribbon Beagles.

Dr. William Lamar Stabler in 1945 with the horse his father gave him in 1941. Doc has practiced veterinary medicine in Houston since November 1949. His wife, Wilma Elaine "Southern" Stabler provides much support for her husband.

Groundbreaking for the "Community House" at corner of Dulaney and Pearl Street in Houston, MS. Opal Gore and Lee Horn with shovels. Children are ? and Steve Roebuck. Back, L-R: Mrs. E.F. White, Gladys Worden, Mildred Harris, Bill Smith, Marianne Metts, Jack Page, Mattie Moore, Lucille Dulaney, Harry Vickery, Elkin Dendy, Virginia Marion, Lucille Dendy, Otis Beasley, Mrs. J.W. Hill, Katherine Roebuck and Robyn Horn.

Foreground, L-R: Ludie Harrington, Joan Lowry, Doss Lowry and Levi Harrington at Luther Harrington's pool.

Laverne Guest Cook and daughter Mary Jo Guest on what is now County Road 39 in the Thorn Community, 1946.

Jack Hill riding his bike to school in 1946, East Hamilton Street, Houston (in front of present home of Jimmy and Betty Smith).

Right: Vardaman (Boozie) Sanderson from Chickasaw County, receiving certificate for six years as doorman of the Mississippi Senate, no absences, no tardies.

L.C. Hobson store in Houlka; Curry Hobson is on the right.

Scenes from the Wilson Park in Okolona, MS, 1940s.

Joyce Gann Naron is in the drivers seat of Gene Harrington's Roadster. Standing L-R is Don Harrington, Mae Helen Gann Nelson and Dot Gann Wilson.

Service Station located at the present site of City Hall in Houston, 1951. In the background is the side of old Tabb Drug Store building. Various business were located upstairs, including Miss Tressie Berry's Beauty Shop.

Winston Reeves, Sue Fleming and Winnie Ruth Landreth at Davis Lake, 1952.

Elizabeth Thompson Gann and Dorothy Ann Gann Wilson with Sylvester at the "8 Drive-In."

L-R: Helen Tramel, Dr. Henry Lee and Laquita James Martin, in front of the old Houston Hospital, 1952.

Laquita James Martin, Dr. John D. Dyer and ? McLaughlin from New Albany, Houston Hospital, May 1952.

Hulet Hobson and Dr. J.M. Hood outside Dr. Hood's office in Houlka, Mississippi.

Homer Sharp by his "telephone truck."

How it was in Ed Lloyd's pool hall in 1954. Note the method for keeping snooker scores near the ceiling. L-R: Ed Lloyd, Mac Smith, Charles Moore, Jesse Foster and T.F. Millsaps.

Mae Helen Gann Nelson and Sara Hardin at the switchboard of Southern Bell Telephone Office in 1954 or 1955.

Southern Bell Telephone Co. operators, 1955. Front L-R: Rose Sisk, daughter Sharon Sisk on Frances Moore's lap and Betty J. Hill (Smith). Back row is Doris Hardin (West Point operator) Dell Harrington, Sara Hardin, Al Anglin.

Houston's participants in the Ted Mack Amatuer Hour, Memphis, Tennessee, November 1955. Back row, L-R: Trent Wood, Jeannette Park, Julia Faye Shempert, Linda Wilson, Ann Worden, Judy Kyle, Bennett Blanton. Front row L-R: Carolyn and Linda Griffin, Norma Tillman, Bill Patch and unidentified.

Looking east on Main Street in Okolona in the 1950s.

Shirley Carroll Mathis and Carolyn Carroll Skelton with Elvis Presley after his performance at Bruce High School in 1955.

L-R: Frances Corley, Mag Julia Jaggers and Mary Lou Pullen working the Okolona Telephone Exchange before its closure in 1956.

93

L-R: Kay Young (Griffin) and Josephine Peden (Higginbotham) with their "can-can" slips under control, visit with James (Hardrock) Criddle and James Wm. Duke on the square in Houlka, 1958.

Ben Wilson, "The Barber of Pyland" cuts Wilton Johnson's hair, 1959.

Sally Shearer Smith, RN, checking charts at the desk on the third floor of the old Houston Hospital on North Jackson Street.

A group from Chickasaw County at Columbus Air Force Base, 1961. L-R: Derwood McCullough, Willie Foster, T/Sgt. James Smith, Clyde Berry, ?, Deward Lester, Devan Hill, James Hardin, Arthur Quinn, Everett Griffin, Doyle McQuary, Calvin Lancaster, Robert Atkinson, Ollie Kimbrough, Dave Westmoreland, Johnny Murphree, Doss Lowry, Col. Jim Morrison, Charles Tillman, Armis Hawkins, W.W. Brand, Sr. and Sid Harris.

John Harvey Allen's badge from the Gulf Ordnance Plant at Prairie, MS.

No passenger train stops at Houlka's delapidated train station, but in another day, it would have been a beehive of activity.

Robert A. Stewart retired December 31, 1965, after 45 $\frac{1}{2}$ years as a rural mail carrier.

Scarlette and Debra Pumphrey with local celebrity, Bobbie Gentry.

Sisters Coila Wilson Thompson, Gladys Wilson House and Lena Wilson Lancaster during one of their many days of quilting together.

Opal Dendy Gore, as a volunteer, helps Mr. Emmitt Ausley (93 years of age) in the summer of 1972.

Back L-R: Jack Earnest, great-great-grandson of Thomas Jefferson Lowry, his mother, Louise Lowry Earnest and husband Ed Earnest. Front row: L-R: fifth generation descendants of T.J. Lowry, early minister of Prospect United Methodist Church.

EVENTS WE'VE CELEBRATED

Claude and Jennie Weaver Melton on their wedding day, 1903 or 1904.

Myrtie Clara Scarbrough (1888-1983) probably on her wedding day in 1904 when she married James Edward Dendy.

Ezekiel Thomas Moore and Sevella Higginbotham Moore, married February 26, 1911.

Allen and Essie Fortner Johnson's wedding picture; they were married in the buggy.

4th of July Picnic at the Thorn School House, date unknown. To the right of the flagholder is Mary McCluney Wilson, to his left is Bessie McCluney Thomas.

Roy Alton Rhodes and Minnie Ethel Brown on their wedding day, December 12, 1921.

1936 Centennial Celebration of Houston - Board of Supervisors L-R: J. Ed Dendy, Earl Anderson, Franks Doss, Jesse Alford and Charles E. Chrestman. Front left is Elizabeth Dendy Patch, 4th from left is Wilma Farned Sigler.

Nurses from the Houston Hospital ride on a float in Houston's Centennial Celebration in 1936.

It's Houston's 100th birthday in 1936. On the Houston Coca Cola Bottling Co. float, going up Pontotoc Street, are from L-R: Joann Ray (Craig), Joan Blissard, Nancy Carol Davis (Storey) and Jane Hodges (Bowles) in her Shirley Temple dress. S.U. Hodges was manager of the Coca Cola plant and the company celebrated it's 50th anniversary. The house in the background is still lived in today.

Homecoming Day at Thorn Church of God in late 1930s.

From left: Bill Reedy, Frank Reedy, Keet and Mack Abbott, Jack Weaver and Jennie Weaver Melton.

It's 1944 and Robert O. Kendall (Bob-o) and Carleen McCluney share birthdays, but not cake, in Pyland. He is 6 and she is 1.

Rev. Jake Nabors and wife Anna Higginbotham Nabors on their 50th wedding anniversary.

Lee Edgar Wooldridge and wife, Margaret Zelda Lowery on their 50th anniversary in 1952.

Annie Lee G. Kendall and the new Mr. and Mrs. Robert Hawkins Kendall at the Flight 21 Restaurant, Houston.

"Dinner on the Ground" at the Langley home place in Thorn; Will, Sally and Ella Langley in 1953.

Hugh J. and Rachel Waldrop Wilson, seated between sons Ollie and Hollie, at their 65th wedding anniversary, December 1953. Standing are children Louise McCullough, Aubrey Wilson, Roberta Naron Parkman, Gladys House, Coila Thompson and Lena Lancaster.

50th wedding anniversary of Marion Monroe and Rosa Jennings McQuary, December 1954. Seven of their children are in the picture.

Minnie Jo Beaty and Roy Edward Hill married June 6, 1956.

Wedding of Betty Joan Gordon and Woodrow Wilson Brand, Jr., August 1956. From left: James E. (Jim) Gordon, Lottie Gordon, Gus Gordon, Betty Gordon, Woodrow Brand, Jr., Woodrow W. Brand, Sr., Nancy Lane Brand, Cornelia Brand and Ann Brand.

The September 11, 1956, wedding of Elizabeth "Libba" Rogers and Joseph E. "Joe" Criddle at Pleasant Ridge Baptist Church. L-R: Gilbert Daniel, soloist; John Scott "Scotty" Ross, usher; Lottie Rogers Corley, matron of honor; the bride and groom; Walter Evans Gann, best man; Martha Rose Lancaster, bridesmaid; Clayton Corley, the bride's brother-in-law who gave her away; and Willadean Daniel Teague, pianist. The ceremony was performed by the bride's father, Bro. Jep E. Rogers, standing between the bride and groom.

Mr. Bailey of Bell Telephone of Tupelo and Ms. Mary Foster upon her retirement and the closing of the Okolona Telephone office, about 1956.

L-R: "Mug" Finn serves as best man for Byron Lamar Wilson with his bride, Dorothy Ann Gann. Standing with her is Jo Ann Clark Herrod. Minister is Rev. Odis Henderson. May 25, 1957.

Grady and Mary Williams at the beginning, 1961.

Helen Ruth Wilson and Robert Oren Kendall, just married at the Immaculate Heart of Mary Catholic Church, October 26, 1962.

Left: Front row, L-R: Lelon, Claudie (Shorty) and Granville Melton. Back row, L-R: Syble, Maudie, Annie, Claude, Jennie, Macie, Audie and Josie Melton.

Right: Emma Starnes Hill on her 90th birthday at the home of her daughter, Mrs. Pauline (Everett) Griffin.

100

"Bobbie Gentry Day" in Chickasaw County. She's wearing a complimentary blue dress from Dendy's Dept. Store in Houston. In her song Papa, Won't you let me go to Town was the line "There's a blue dress in Dendy's."

50th wedding anniversary of J.W. and Elvia Hatley in 1964. Front L-R: William "Buddy" Hatley, J.D., Wilburn and Lester Hatley. Back row: Rena Hatley Criddle Harmon, John and Elvia Guyton Hatley, Inez H. Elliott, Neomie H. Riley and Lola M. Hatley.

Ronald D. Morris received his Eagle Scout award January 1974. Pictured here with Scoutmaster Bob Dendy and his mother, Martha Morris.

Howard and Doris Wooldridge Kellum at their 50th anniversary, February 15, 1975. L-R: Barbara Melton, Robert Melton, Darlene Kellum, Gary Kellum, Doris, Howard, Colleen Smith, Bob Smith, Jessie Kellum, Charles Kellum, Bobbie Pumphrey and W.L. Pumphrey.

Helping to Celebrate America's 200th birthday in Chickasaw County, MS, July 1976 is Overton James, the governor of the Chickasaw Nation of Oklahoma, his wife, mother, daughter and granddaughter.

Lillie Mae Hawkins Kendall and Robert Clifton Kendall on their 60th wedding anniversary, June 1976.

Judge Woodrow W. Brand, Jr. speaks at the Bicentennial Celebration in July 1976, Pinson Square in Houston.

Mr. and Mrs. Preston Williams on their 50th wedding anniversary, February 7, 1977.

Talley Anderson (Cooper) (1958-1987) shared the same birthday with her grandfather, Charlie Anderson (1895-1982).

Children, grandchildren and great-grandchildren of Daniel Foster Wilson's marriages to Modera Verell and Katie Cox; summer of 1978 at Enon Primitive Baptist Church.

Mr. and Mrs. Raymond Wolter, October 1980. The bride is the former Betsy Gordon Brand.

50th wedding anniversary of Richard (Dick) and Dolly Westbrook Nelson, May 1978. L-R: Jewel Palmer Tisdell, John Nelson, Dora Nelson Coggins, Jim Dick Nelson, Dick Nelson, David Nelson, Dolly Westbrook Nelson, Nancy Nelson Drummond, Oliver Nelson, Bonnie Nelson Buskirk, Margaret Jo Nelson Johnson and Betty Nelson Dean.

Dr. and Mrs. Woodrow W. Brand III, July 27, 1985. The bride is the former Melinda Lee Garner.

Curt and Estelle Law of Houlka at their 50th wedding anniversary, October 1986.

50th Reunion of the Class of 1937. Standing, L to R: Willie Foster, Bill Patch, Allie Scott George and Nig Patch; Seated L - R: Mildred Medlin Scott, Martha Medlin Shepherd, Hazel Crans and Mack Priest.

The Houston High School Class of 1937, with some spouses, as it looked 50 years later. Seated L to R: Mack Priest, Mildred M. Scott and Grace Foster. Standing L to R: Frances D. Priest, Nig Patch, Bill Patch, A.G. Shepherd, Jr., Martha Shepherd, Harold Carty and Willie Foster.

Friends congratulate Mrs. B.H. (Margaret) Baine on her 100th birthday, January 1988.

Miller Clark on his 100th birthday with his sister Eunice Wooldridge who was 97 at the time.

Lottie Kilgore Earnest (left) and twin, Ottie Kilgore Criddle celebrate their 80th birthday.

Mr. and Mrs. Sid Dendy at their 50th wedding anniversary.

Nashville, Tennessee, 1995. Tim McGraw in hat, Marcus Hall to his left, Jeb Anderson of Okolona to his left, Steve Dukes to his left. Hall, Anderson and Dukes were co-writers of McGraw's hit song "I Like It, I Love It."

Billy Wayne Duncan, L.C. Duncan, Johnnie Duncan, Pam Vaughn, Myra Reeves and Sheila Webster at L. C. and Johnnie's 45 wedding anniversary, December 24, 1996.

Standing L-R: Douglas Langley, Sara L. Chase, Ruth L. Griffin, Bill Langley, Bobby Langley and Harley Langley. Seated L-R: Lorette Wheeler, Johnnie Duncan, L.C. Duncan and Lois Langley at Johnnie and L.C.'s 45 anniversary, December 1996.

SCENES FROM BYGONE DAYS

Carl Cook on his farm in the Chalk Bluff Community, early 1900s.

Charley Neal in his conveyance of the day.

Roy Ruble Davis about 1910-1912.

Frank King, Gibson, MS, in 1911. Husband of Susie Chandler King.

Shirley Hawkins Harrington and her father, Joe L. Hawkins, crossing the Mississippi River on a ferry, about 1917.

Ray Wooldridge came in a buggy to court Eunice Clark (seated in buggy). Connie Brown teasingly caught the horses reins and wouldn't let them leave. Ray and Eunice were married Feb. 23, 1919 and lived in Thorn. Ray died 1974, Eunice died at 103 in 2002.

Lester Hampton bought one of the first Chevrolets made. His son, Featherston Hampton is sitting on the fender. Inside is Lester, Tom Mitchell, Curt Robertson and Worth Darby, 1919. There were more wagon trails than roads.

Dr. J.M. Hood with an unidentified passenger, 1920.

Allen Johnson and the car that took him from Mantee to Marks, MS, on two gallons of gas. He swapped paint for more gas.

Lawrence Harrington, driver for the A.C. Harrington Co., the first bus-taxi service in Houston. This bus picked up passengers at depot and delivered them to their destination. Picture made about 1920.

Guy Smith and his sister, Susie Mae, in front of the team, hitched and ready.

The Dendy "School Bus"

L-R: Edgar House, daughters Mayrene House (Bullock) and Lynette House (Gann) and wife Gladys Wilson House. Circa 1922-23.

"At the front door" parking; east side of Courthouse, Houston.

Jim Alexander holding Kenneth "Buck" Davis in a 1924 Ford Coupe.

Rush Hall Robertson and a 1926 Chevrolet.

Ruby Moore Rucker, her son E.B. and daughter Mary Ruth in front of Ruby's father's (Ezekiel T. Moore) first car bought in the early 1930s.

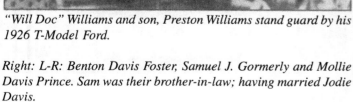

"Will Doc" Williams and son, Preston Williams stand guard by his 1926 T-Model Ford.

Right: L-R: Benton Davis Foster, Samuel J. Gormerly and Mollie Davis Prince. Sam was their brother-in-law; having married Jodie Davis.

James Dulaney by the Dulaney Hardware Co. delivery truck.

Ida Hobson standing by friend's Model T Ford.

1936 Chevrolet

Russell Kendall, son Robert (Bob) Kendall and niece Laura Rogers stand in front of "Leapin' Lena," the 1937 Ford Coupe (flat-head V8 engine and a 3-speed in the floor) that Russell, "Shorty" Rogers and J.W. Riley raced on the dirt track in Tupelo.

Lex Wilson, center, is presented a check from the Exchange Club by J.S. Hickman. The Lex Wilson-Doss Lowry Jersey cattle operation was awarded first prize. On the left is Dolph Montgomery, third place winner. May 1937.

The pick-up used by Simpson's Grocery to deliver groceries to the residents of Houston.

Martin Cook holding Nancy Jo Cook on his hay-raker, Thorn Community, 1938.

Samuel Guy Smith

Lorena Ashley Duke with grandchildren Jeannette Park (Stevens) and Roland Duke seated on the running board of a pickup in 1939.

Cotton crop at Thorn, MS, date unknown. L to R: Charles Edward McCluney, Ellen S. McCluney, Unknown Brantley, Lora Brantley McCluney and Jim Brantley.

Granville Melton and Coley Mooneyham Melton; note his initials on front of the car.

Left: The Cotton Yard in Okolona, 1930s, near the present Compress Building.

Bedford Hobson and his horse, Jake.

Doss Lowry's truck in 1940 when he worked for Kraft Cheese. The sign refers to his job of encouraging farmers to raise more crops.

Red Sanderson holds an "oat cradle" that was used to cut oats.

L-R: Betty, Jerrell and Sue Fleming, taken in the Reid Community, Christmas of 1940.

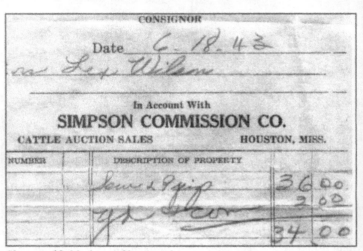

She was $9.00 short of having the money to pay property taxes, her husband is in the Sanitorium at McGee, MS. Mrs. Lex (Sydney H.) Wilson sells a sow and 9 baby pigs for $36.00 less yardage and commission of $2.00.

Durell Gann and daughter Joyce clean their 1940 Ford.

John A. Lowry in the fall of 1944. T-Model Ford bought from a Mr. Wicker whose wife ran a boarding house at present site of True-Value Hardware.

Nash car owned by Oda Hobson Neal and husband, Rev. W.R. Neal.

Dr. S.K. and Cora Scarbrough Gore

It's the early 1940s and Juanice Neal (Grant), Doxie Davis and Dorothy Neal (Martino) are going for a ride.

Small Cub tractor of A.J. Harrington, Jr. used on his family farm at Sonora.

Earvin Claude "Shelley" Brand (1875-1955), son of Wm. Perry and Margaret Hinds Brand, with granddaughter Joyce Brand Porter in a mid 1940s buggy ride with the help of Peanut. Mr. Shelley had a whip that he used on most of the boys of "Hot Air" when they ran after his buggy.

Howard Hugh Smith gets assistance from Vickie Huffman Barnett in pushing an old Studebaker automobile.

Leon Neal has hitched up two mules to his wagon and is about to take daughters Marie Neal (Sheffield) and twins Molly Neal (Johnson) and Sally Neal (Beaty) with him.

Otha Foster Sr. (right front) and three unidentified men cook out sorghum molasses.

William J.B. Scott and mules, Kate and Tige about 1946.

After WW II, C.E. "Dick" Griffin (1918-1992 son of Presley Edgar and Lizzie Gann Griffin) returned to farming in 1946 with these mules. The mules were stubborn, so Dick went to work for the U.S. Forestry Service and worked there 30 years.

James Eldridge Park, 1948

Charles Aaron Martin and his old Ford.

Lizzie Gann Griffin Harmon in front of an early 1950s Chevrolet.

It's haying time in Pyland, MS. Annie Lee Kendall stands by Lynn Kendall who is seated on the tractor; Russell Kendall, with shovel, is behind the tractor; Robert C. Kendall (Bob), Zeb (June) Philpot and Robert Oren (Bob-o) Kendall atop the hay.

Doss Lowry in his fescue/clover pasture in May, 1950.

Cecil R. Williams in a typical rural scene, 1954.

C.C. (Cap) Mixon using his mule "Wild Bill" to break up his garden in the spring.

John Lowry combining fescue with the first self-propeled combine in the county, a Massey-Ferguson.

Hardin Davis at a sorghum mill in the mid 1950s.

Bud Langley in cotton patch in Thorn, late 1950s.

Ronnie (left) and Jimmie Cook washing sweet potatoes the only way it was done in 1964.

Lois, Bud, Bobby Vaughn and Douglas Langley in their garden at Thorn, 1961.

Charlie Carter (left) and Roy Cook hampering sweet potatoes in the Thorn Community, 1963.

Walter Chandler and his antique 1949 Chevrolet pick-up truck

Typical of the early methods of delivering freight, Vance & Son Freight Co.'s wagon pulled by a team of oxen.

OFFICIALS FROM OUR COUNTY

Left: Anderson Bean (1804-1896) and wife Ann Caroline Garrett (1807-1895) of the Buena Vista Community. He served as one of the early sheriffs of Chickasaw County, MS.

Right: Jodie Lewis Davis (1875-1957) served as Chickasaw County Circuit Clerk for two terms and as Sheriff and Tax Collector in the early 1900s.

Chickasaw County Board of Supervisors about 1908-1912. Top L-R: Hal Brannon, Chancery Clerk; J.A. Trenor, Beat 3; Sid E. Atkinson, Beat 1; possibly Nedford Gann, Beat 4. Bottom L-R: Jack Wilson, Beat 5; possibly John M. Stone; John Winter, Beat 2. Possibly included in picture would be N.W. Bradford, attorney and/or T. W. Hamilton, clerk.

First grand jury to meet in the new courthouse, about 1909-10.

Chickasaw County officials 1912-1916. Bottom L-R: Frank Walker, Tax Assessor; Hal Brannon, Chancery Clerk; Joe L. Davis, Circuit Court Clerk; Jeff Busby, County Attorney; Jess Nabors, County Treasurer; George Riley, Supt. of Education and Henry Harrington, Sheriff and Tax Collector.

Left: Jeff Busby as a candidate for U.S. Congress in 1922. He served from 1922-1935.

Right: Dennis Murphree, son of Alice Pilgreen Murphree of Okolona, served three times as Lt. Gov. From 1924-27; 1932-36 and 1940-43. He filled the Governor's chair on two occasions due to the death of the Governor.

Chickasaw County Board of Supervisors, at Houston's Centennial celebration in 1936. L-R: Franks Doss, Charles E. Chrestman, Jesse Alford, Earl Anderson and J. Ed Dendy.

Left: Burks Davis, Houston's Water Superintendent during the 1920s and 1930s; father of Frances Priest and Buck Davis. Middle: William Hugh Johnson (1895-1941) first Game Warden in Chickasaw County; married to Mae Lorene Ford; father of Alta Mae Johnson Wagnon Hardin, James Ford Johnson, Dorothy Lucille Johnson Baine, Mary Bell Johnson Cooper Meyer, Martha Ann Johnson Sumner, Ella Hughes Johnson McCullough and Billie Grace Johnson Blair. Photo made about 1939.

Right: Jim Alexander, Houston Chief of Police for a number of years and Chickasaw County Sheriff from 1957 to 1960. Photo made 1941. Man on left is ? Dilloworth.

L-R: Odie Trenor, John Hugh Simpson, Elliott Parker, ?, and B. Smith in the courthouse at Houston, year unknown.

Chickasaw County Department of Public Welfare workers, March 20, 1940. L-R: Mrs. J.C. Hightower, Assistant Agent; Mrs. George Bean, Agent; Mary Lowe Kirby and Mary Dulaney, workers; Mable Smith, secretary and Mildred Medlin, worker.

Left: Thomas G. Abernethy of Okolona, served as U.S. Congressman from 1943 to 1973.

Middle: Tom Scarbrough was Sheriff of Chickasaw County from 1945-1948; later served as State Highway Commissioner.

Right: Roy Paden Davis, Chief of Police

117

CITY OF HOUSTON MAYORS

1961-2002

Mayor John A. (Pap) Moore
2001-2005
(Current Administration)

Mayor W.W. Brand Jr.
1961-1970

Houston is a healthy and hospitable city in NE Mississippi that gained its "Hallmark" in history and heritage of this area by harnessing all of the setbacks that halter progress and by its civic leaders exerting a lot or work, planned progress, and harmony.

The city was well-named after a real historic hustler, Sam Houston, in 1836, who, at that time, was President of the Republic of Texas.

Many capable leaders have guided the steps of infant Houston to the grown-up city it is today. It is only fitting and proper that we remember and honor here the mayors from the last forty years. Two of the last seven mayors are now deceased, Mayor John J. Bentz and Mayor R.H. Verell.

Mayor W.D. (Bill) Smith
1993-2001

Mayor John J. Bentz
1970-1973

Mayor James M. (Jimmy) Smith
1985-1993

Mayor R.H. (Bob) Verell
1977-1982

Mayor Harry G. Robinson
1973-1977
1982-1985

WELCOME TO
HOUSTON, MISSISSIPPI

INCORPORATED IN 1836   **2000 POPULATION 4079**

Citizens involved in the improvement of our city.

MS Valley Flywheel Festival; Joe Brigance Park; April and September of each year; Over 10,000 attendants.

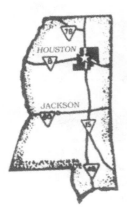

Houston Carnegie Libary, Mississippi's first Carnegie Library; Established in 1909; Over 16,000 books checked out annually; 4 internet connections.

2001-2005
CURRENT ADMINISTRATION

Left: Chief of Police Kevin A. Davis (1997-2005)

Right: Mayor John A. (Pap) Moore (2001-2005) and Aldermen. From left: Thomas E. Griffin (2110-2005), Shenia Kirby-Jones (1989-2005), Leon Martin (1984-2005), Mayor Moore, Brenda Crawford (1985-2005), Stacey W. Parker (2001-2005).

Kid's Park, Place where wishes come true! Completed in five days - March 2000

A tribute to our favorite big leaguers, approximately 400 youth.

Grady Chenault, City Marshall of Okolona, MS, 1934-1961.

Charles William "Charlie" Anderson, Sr., Chickasaw County Sheriff, 1936-1940

Thomas Jefferson Lowry, son of Elizabet Doss and Alfred Rushing Lowry; Highway Commissioner for Northern District, 1940-1948.

Justice Court Judge "Mose" Johnson, Okolona, MS, early 1950s.

Doyle McQuary, Chickasaw County School Superintendent, in foreground.

Morgan Davis on left and Chickasaw County Supervisor Armstrong Farr evaluate the widening of a road.

Judge Brown; Dolly Nabors, Deputy Clerk; and Ralph Thomas, Chickasaw County Circuit Clerk.

The first women jurors in Chickasaw County, Mississippi. Jodie Gormerly at far left, Florence Coburn next; others unidentified.

CHICKASAW COUNTY

HOUSTON   HOULKA   OKOLONA   WOODLAND

Acquired from the Chickasaw Indians by the Treaty of Pontotoc Creek, the present area known as Chickasaw County became part of the United States in 1832. In 1836, four months after Chickasaw County was officially established, efforts began that led to the establishment of the City of Houston. Property offered by Joel Pinson was accepted as the county seat and became what is now Houston, named after Pinson's friend, Major General Sam Houston.

As Chickasaw County grew, settlers experienced difficulty traveling to Houston (the county seat) from the eastern side of Chuquantonchee Creek. To combat this problem, special legislation was passed making Okolona, located on the eastern side of the Chuquantonchee, a second county seat.

Exclusive things you will find in Chickasaw County are:
- The Carnegie Library - Mississippi's first, established in 1909 in Houston
- The Confederate Soldiers' Cemetery - Civil War burial site in Okolona
- The Tombigbee National Forest - approximately 28,000 acres in Chickasaw County
- Camp Tik-a-Witha - Girl Scout Camp located at Van Vleet
- The Chickasaw County Fair - Memorable and traditional family fun
- The Natchez Trace Parkway - a two-lane, scenic highway offering natural beauty in every season
- Davis Lake - 200 acre lake with outstanding fishing, boating, camping and hiking
- City of Lights - Each Christmas, Houston transforms into the City of Lights. Thousands of white lights are draped from the courthouse dome and engulf the town square and surrounding buildings.

Chickasaw County Board of Supervisors: Lonnie Whitt, Board President; Wilson Kirby; David Vance; Ricko Nickols; Russell Brooks.

Left: Chickasaw County Officials, 2002: Sandra Willis, Circuit Court; David Thomas, Chancery Clerk; Dale Mooneyham, Tax Assessor; John A. Gregory, County Attorney; Jimmy Simmons, Sheriff.

L-R: Mississippi Governor Ross Barnett, Senator Robert D. "Bob" Anderson of Okolona and Senator Raymond Bailey of Calhoun County. 1962

A gathering of Chickasaw County officials on the courthouse steps. Front, L to R: Chancerk Clerk Derwood McCullough, Supervisors Robert Atkinson and Lloyd Collums. Rear L-R: Supervisors Parker Lancaster, Calvin Lancaster, DeVan Hill and Circuit Clerk Clyde A. "Shifty" Berry.

Chickasaw County Sheriff's Department, 1976. L-R: Lloyd Eaton, Sheriff; Andrew Lyles, Deputy; Roger Oswalt, Chief Deputy; Toby Craig, Deputy; Fred Clark, Deputy; and Margaret Ann Peel, Deputy.

Left; Presidential candidate Jimmy Carter's "Peanut Brigade" bus at its stop in Houston.

Right: William E. (Billy) Bowles, State Representative from District 22. First elected in 1984, he still serves in this capacity. He is a resident of the Thorn Community.

THREE GENERATIONS OF HOUSTON CITY MARSHALS

Roy Ruble Davis
Houston Town Marshal, 1929-1931

Roy Paden Davis
Houston City Marshal, 1953-1982

Kevin Adams Davis
Houston City Marshal, 1997-present

Badges of the office...

Pompey Davis on duty.

The badge of
Roy Ruble Davis

The badge of
Kevin Adams Davis

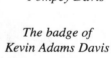

The badge of
Pompey Davis

Kevin Adams Davis
Directing school traffic

The Davis family of Houston has a longstanding history of serving the city of Houston. Three generations have served as city marshal: Roy Ruble Davis, from 1929-1931; Roy Paden "Pompey" Davis, from 1953-1982; and Kevin Adams Davis, from 1997-present. Roy Ruble succeeded T.H. Pope as Town Marshal. At that time the term of office was two years and Roy Ruble was defeated in his second attempt by J.H. Alexander. Only seven years old at that time, young "Pompey" Davis vowed to run against, and defeat the Marshal and Tax Collector who defeated his father. In 1953 Pompey did defeat Mr. Alexander, ending Alexander's 22-year career.

Pompey's first term as City Marshal marked the beginning of four-year terms. He would go on to serve seven full 4-year terms and a year of the 8th term, resigning only when failing health forced him out of office. Pompey was the first Houston City Marshal to wear a uniform, and to require his staff to be uniformed. He started the position with a night-watchman as staff, but by 1978 had 5 uniformed officers and 4 radio operators. He began directing school traffic upon taking office in 1953, and maintained an exemplary record of zero school-traffic fatalities in his 29 years of service. Pompey suffered a stroke in September of 1981, and although he tried to continue to work, he soon realized it was time to pass the torch.

At the time of Pompey's retirement, his youngest child, Kevin Adams Davis was serving in the United States Navy. It would be another 16 years before Kevin would take on the uniform of his father. In July of 1997, following retirement from the Navy and after being on the Houston Police Force two years, Kevin Adams Davis was elected Houston's City Marshal. Kevin continues the tradition of directing school traffic. He has instituted a policy requiring all officers to pass a minimum training and physical fitness test. Like his father and grandfather before him, Kevin dedicates his life daily to the safety of Houston residents.

January 3, 1981 - Armis E. Hawkins is sworn in as Justice of the Mississippi Supreme Court by Justice Kermit Cofar. Over his shoulder at extreme left is Charlie Hawkins, brother to the new Justice.

Devan Hill and wife Doris of Okolona, MS. Devan Hill served as supervisor from District 3 from 1948 to 1992. At the time of his election in 1947, he was the youngest supervisor in the state.

Harold Stevens, District 3 Supervisor with Derwood McCullough, former Chickasaw County Chancery Clerk on right, 1994.

Elected Chancery Judge in December of 1998, James S. Gore is pictured with his family after taking the oath of office.

Chancery Judge James S. Gore administers the oath of office to the 2000 Board of Supervisors. L-R: Wilson Kirby, Ricko Nichols, Russell Brooks, Harold Stevens and Lonnie Whitt.

CHURCHES

Rev. Wesley Fletcher Patch and his wife, Lille May, July 11, 1900. He served as pastor of Presbyterian churches in Chickasaw County in the 1930s and 40s.

Men's Bible Class, Methodist Church in Houston, about 1912; Mrs. R.P. Neblett, teacher.

Mantee Baptist Church Singing School, date unknown, teacher was "Mr. Hooker."

Bethel Baptist Church, second building which served from 1889-1952. Date of picture unknown.

Baptist Men's Sunday School Class, abt. 1927. Bottom L-R W. D. Stewart, W.A. Harrington, D.A. Goza, R.M. Chenault, S.D. Goza, M.V. Chenault, T.H. Pope and Mrs. J.C. Beasley. 2nd L-R: Charley Brown, J.E. Dendy, J.F. Woodruff, W.O. Huddleston, D.M. Hearn, Roland Kirby, Early Woodruff, Mr. Brooks, Clay Beason, Will Canipe. 3rd L-R: J.H. Ford, Russell Ingram, H.L. Harrington, Byron Smith, ?, Cedric Dendy. 4th L-R: J.C. Davis, L.L. Goza, J.C. Paden, Felix Rutledge, John Rhodes, A.D. Harrington, L.A. Harrington

and R.E. Goza. 5th L-R: Will Parker, E.J. Hall, James T. Blair, F.W. Byars, J.O. Hightower, W.A. Wilkinson. 6th L-R: E.F. White, Lee Horn, B.F. Lyles, Orie Verell, C.O. Trenor, John E. Davis and J.W. Hamilton.

Wesley Chapel Methodist Church, founded in 1851, still serves a congregation at its original location North of Houston.

The second building to serve as Enon Primitive Baptist Church, erected in 1906 and used until a brick structure was built in 1967. Enon was organized in 1886. Elder C.E. Couch was the first church clerk; Elder E.M. Verell served as first pastor.

New Hope Church of God-Apostolic Faith - in the old Martin School Building; L-R B.K. Moss, W.W. Blissard, Lola Welch, W.N. (Bud) Gore, Homie Blissard and Ruth Huffman. Child Maynard Huffman with Shirley Moss.

Pleasant Ridge Baptist Church, ca 1960. Bro. Jep E. Rogers pastored here from 1955-1960 and led in building the two-story educational building shown here on the right.

Left: Bro. Jep Rogers and wife Mamie Martin Rogers at Pleasant Ridge Church, where he served from 1955-1960. From there he went to Starkville, MS, and died there March 7, 1961. Mamie returned to Okolona and lived there until her death, Christmas Day, 1999.

First Baptist Church, Okolona; erected 1924.

First United Methodist Church, Okolona; erected 1908.

Groundbreaking in 1949 for the First United Methodist Church, North Jackson Street, Houston, MS.

Vacation Bible School, 1954, at the Saxon Memorial Church of the Nazarene, Houston, MS.

Final stages of construction of the Immaculate Heart of Mary Catholic Church, Houston, MS; completed in 1954.

William Flenoy Clark, "Brother Flenoy," born 1913, died 1978.

Rev. Ben McGhee and wife, Flora.

127

United Methodist Church Choir, early 1960s. All L-R: Front: Mrs. C.K. Alexander, Organist; Katherine McLeroy, Director; Mrs. Corinne Ray, Pianist. First Row: Mary Ann Alford, Catherine Davis, Joyce Forrest, Rose Revel, Lesbya Griffin, Robyn Horn, Elease Miller, Tommie Davis and Joann Craig. Middle: Ruth Turner, Betty Wright, Julia Bowles, Pearline Crawford, Mabel Wessels, Irlene Dulaney and Maureen Norman. Back: John Brand, Bob Baldwin, Fred McIntosh, Perry White, Gene Russell, E.C. Webber, Robert Lee Crawford, Roy Harmon and Willie Foster.

Egypt Baptist Church, formed in the 1840s.

Getting ready for "Dinner on the Ground," third Sunday in April 1973, at Enon Primitive Baptist Church. Sydney H. Wilson on left. Meda Wilson Morton White looks on with Iota Verell and Catherine Wilson Walls.

Bro. Terry Burnside, founder of Faith Bible Church in Houston in 1977. Pictured in 1985 with his wife, Phyllis and children Terri, Patrick and Phillip.

Singing "Ole' Harp" at Enon Primitive Baptist Church, east of Houston. Charles Porter, at left, leads the singing. Byron Wilson and George Easley in front of the pulpit.

Left: Senior Citizen Day at the Shiloh Baptist Church, July 13, 1986, Houlka, MS. Front L-R Gertrude Gann, Lorena Duke, Edith McCullough, Emma Johnson, Grace Barnette. Back L-R: Rudell Eddington, Curt Barnette, Irene Holms, Maylene Edington.

CLUBS AND ORGANIZATIONS

4-H Club, Houston, MS, 1928. Far right end on front row is Bulldog Baird.

L-R: Harvey Lee Morrison, Pat McKinley, Abb Crump, Charlie Anderson, George Bean and John Stone are among a group receiving the "First V Award" in Jackson, MS, in September of 1944 for bond buying by the War Finance Department.

The Jr. Twentieth Century Club, (later the Cosmopolitan Club) in 1952. Seated L-R: Harriet Pearson, Jane Bowles, Dot Davis, Dorothy Bush, Lucille Kendall Betts, Frances Harrington Reese. Back L-R: Emma Chatt (Katt), Melba Sanderson, Joyce Aycock, Inez McRoy, Mary Smith, Mary Bagley, Jean McCollum and Ruth Rhodes.

CHICKASAW DEVELOPMENT FOUNDATION

Promoting a positive image of Houston and Chickasaw County for 49 years

Since 1953 the Chickasaw Development Foundation has promoted the economics, industrial, agricultural and commercial development of West Chickasaw County. We salute all the Board Chairmen who have provided the leadership over the past 45 years to make Houston and Chickasaw County what it is today.

Board of Directors 2002

David Thomas
Chairman

Lloyd Eaton
Vice Chairman

Jerry Burgess

Kirkham Dendy

Stacey Parker

Harry Robinson

Sondra Washington

Robert Weaver

Lamar Beaty
Executive Director

George Welch	1953-54	R.H Verell	1973-77
Harry Vickery	1954-56	W.D. Smith III	1977-78
Raymond Rowland	1956-57	Bill Patch	1978-79
Harry Vickery	1957-60	Robbie Dendy	1979-80
Armis Hawkins	1960-61	Charles Carson	1980-81
Dr. C.P. Tillman	1961-62	R.C. Pearson, Jr.	1981-84
T.J. Dendy	1962-63	Leland B. Norman, Jr.	1984-88
R.H Verell	1963-64	Richard Dearman	1988-89
Harrison Upshaw, Jr.	1964-65	Mike Colbert	1989-90
Deedy Harrington	1965-66	Bobby Mooneyham	1990-92
Harold Craig	1966	Roger Mason	1992-94
Armis Hawkins	1966-67	Leland B. Norman, Jr.	1994-96
E.A. Enochs	1967-68	Tom Byrne	1996-97
Robin Mathis	1968-69	James C. Wright	1997-99
Herbert Miller	1969-70	John C. Hall	1999-00
W.D. Smith III	1970-71	Harry G. Robinson	2000-02
Bobby Mooneyham	1971-73	David Thomas	2002-03

BRINGING HISTORY TO HOUSTON WITH THE MISSISSIPPI VALLEY FLYWHEEL FESTIVAL

Blue and Gold Banquet for the Cub Scouts Derby Racing in the mid 1950s. Herman Smith and Wesley Patch were the scout masters.

Okolona Brownie Scouts: Back L-R: Katylee Anderson Brown, ?, Tine Walls, Sally Anderson Azlin, ?, Alice Franks, Alaine Anderson, Coleen Thompson Ray. Front L-R: Laura Stovall, Linda Rosentreter, Patti Stevens, ?, Amy Herrod, Loraine Morgan, Kelli Dickerson and Linda Stovall.

A Girl's Auxillary Coronation at First Baptist Church in Houston, probably mid 1950s.

THE EXCHANGE CLUB OF HOUSTON, MISSISSIPPI

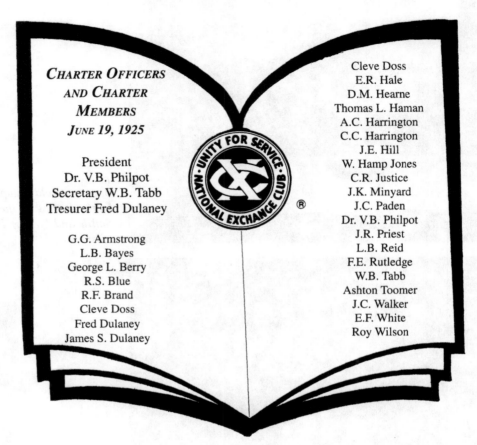

CHARTER OFFICERS AND CHARTER MEMBERS
JUNE 19, 1925

President
Dr. V.B. Philpot
Secretary W.B. Tabb
Tresurer Fred Dulaney

G.G. Armstrong
L.B. Bayes
George L. Berry
R.S. Blue
R.F. Brand
Cleve Doss
Fred Dulaney
James S. Dulaney

Cleve Doss
E.R. Hale
D.M. Hearne
Thomas L. Haman
A.C. Harrington
C.C. Harrington
J.E. Hill
W. Hamp Jones
C.R. Justice
J.K. Minyard
J.C. Paden
Dr. V.B. Philpot
J.R. Priest
L.B. Reid
F.E. Rutledge
W.B. Tabb
Ashton Toomer
J.C. Walker
E.F. White
Roy Wilson

D. Wells Barton, N.B. (Ben) Woods, Mr. ? Block, Dr. V.B. Philpot Sr., John S. Hickman, Sim U. Hodges, W.B. Funderburk, Mr. ? Alford, Walter A. Wilkerson, Ashton Toomer, R.E. (Bob) Atwell, Rev. ? Dawe, Loyce Berry, Charles Miller, unknown, Henry Wilson, Bertram E. Moore, Carter Patch, Turner Ray, Mr. ? Whaley, C.O. Trenor, W.A. Rush, Tom Lester, Rev. W.C. Stewart, Charlie Anderson, John Edgar Hill, Charlie K. Alexander, Cleve Doss, next two unknown, Earl Edwards, Fred Dulaney, Jack Barnes, Dannie Tabb, C.F. Whitaker, Jim Hugh Tabb, Lee Horn, Ed Pearson, Mr. McGowan from Okolona, Dr. G.G. Armstrong, J.H. (Jim) Alexander, unknown, Marvin Boyd, H.D. McMorrow, A.D. Harrington, George Travis (Steve) Roebuck, W.N. Ethridge, Dr. J. Rice Williams, E.F. White, Dr. R.E. Priest, S.F. Smith, unknown, Denton McCluney and Harold Sigler.

John S. Hickman
Ashton Toomer
Harry G. Robinson

Rex F. Sanderson, Past President, Exchange Club Family Center, Oxford, MS, 1998-2002; Harry G. Robinson, Mississippi District President, 2002-2003

2002 MEMBERSHIP

Rex F. Sanderson, W.D. Smith III, Joyce H. East, Harry G. Robinson, Rayburn Parks, Jan Dyson, Hassell Franklin, Robin Mathis, John Lee Lyles, Louis Chandler, Larry Arrington, David Thomas, Roland Oswalt, J.C. Wright, Bob Scott, J.R. Penick, Wallace Norman Jr., Jim Gordon, Gary Murphree, Dale Mooneyham, Rev. Mike Childs, Henry Vaughn, Robert Weaver, Chuck Carson, Max Johnson, Barry Springer, David Horn, Bobby Mooneyham, Tommy Hardin, Dr. Chris Oswalt, Jack Dendy, John Walden, Dr. Raymond Mabry, Lamar Beaty, Loyd Eaton, Dennis Palmer and Charles Chandler.

Left: President Loyd Eaton, 2002-2003; President Wallace Norman Jr., 2001-2002; past presidents.

Right: President Wallace Norman Jr., 2001-2002; David Thomas, Secretary-Treasurer 1979-1999, Treasurer 1999-2002; President Loyd Eaton, 2002-2003; Secretary Joyce East, 1999-2003.

Left: Mrs. Pat Hawkins demonstrating the "Hula" dance for a local club.

Right: Houston Culture Club at their "Easter Parade" in 1965. L-R: Opal Gore, Jimmie Rushing, Nettie Mae Alexander, Rosalyn Eastridge and Corrine Babbs.

The "Colonels" of Gov. J. P. Coleman.

The Thursday Evening Dinner Club (1930-1975). First row L-R: Grace Scott, Estelle Harrington, Minnie Goza, Marianne Metts, Margaret Tindall and Jimmie Rushing. Second row L-R: Frankie Tabb, Katherine McElroy, Virginia McCraine, Corrine Ray, Irlene Dulaney, Catherine Davis, Wilma Hodges and Mary Hickman.

HISTORY OF THE PILOT CLUB OF HOUSTON

1975-76 Pilot Club members. Front to back, from left: Mabelene Easley, Lorene Huffman, Bobbie Nell Pumphrey, Louise Mooneyham, Mildred Martin, Olivia Rhodes, Louise Norman, Virginia Baker, Gertrude Woods, Martha Morris, Jane Bowles, Ira Mae Verell, Nellie Rose Dendy, Jaynell Woodruff.

The Pilot Club of Houston was chartered on February 27, 1964, by the Pilot Club of Tupelo and Pilot International, which is headquartered in Macon, Georgia. The club was presented charter no. 545 and charter members included Geraldine Allen, Mable Cole, Nellie Rose Dendy, Dorothy Nell Dunkin, Jewell Hill, Lorene Huffman, Laverne Johnson, Arline Lewis, Mildred Martin, Norma McAlpin, Louise McCullough, Esterlene McKnight, Louise Norman, Jean Porter, Bobbie Nell Pumphrey, Virginia Rowlett, Ira Mae Verell, Kathleen Wall, Jonnie Weaver Griffin, Ruth Whitt and Gertrude Woods. The charter president of the club was Mrs. Gertrude Woods, with Mrs. Polly Harris, Governor of District III, Winfield, Louisiana, on hand to present the club charter. Internationally, the club's motto is "True Course Ever," the colors are green and gold and the basic principles are "friendship and service." The founders of Pilot International had envisioned an international organization comprised of professional people who would work to improve the quality of life in communities throughout the world by serving those with brain-related disorders and disabilities and other service projects. The name "Pilot" was inspired by the mighty river boat pilots of that day who represented leadership and guidance. The Pilot Wheel is still the recognizable symbol of the organization which boasts over 20,000 members in about 500 clubs in five countries, including the United States, the Bahamas, Canada, Japan and Singapore.

In 1949, PI President Ruby Newhall had the idea of incorporating the same type of civic organization for students. The Anchor Club was established and by 1952, five clubs were organized with the motto, "Anchored We Hold." The Anchor Club turns 50 this year and is open to all students in high schools across the world. The Pilot Club of Houston chartered the Anchor Club of Houston High School on November 22, 1976, with Cara Chisolm and Sandra Langley as faculty advisors. Officers of the chartered club were Mickey Champion, president; Mary Ruth Krieger, vice-president; Jennifer Durden, secretary; Lassie Pickens, treasurer; and directors were Teresa Bonds, Wonda Porter and Rhonda Brand.

Pilot's service focus involves promoting awareness of brain-related disorders and helping those affected through volunteer activities, education and financial support. Pilot works closely with national and international organizations such as the National Organization on Disability, American Heart Association, Dana Alliance for Brain Initiatives, Alzheimer's Association and the Brain Injury Association.

Service projects for the Pilot Club of Houston include: Flag raising at home football games for Houston High School; Sponsor Veteran's Day program; Shoe Boxes for international children at Christmas; Franklin Graham crusade; Drinking and Driving display for Car Safety at holidays; Car seat safety checkpoints with Anchor Club; Annual recognition of Police, Sheriff Department, City workers and Firemen; Floy Dyer Manor birthdays each month (gifts and punch for parties); Annual recognition of Outstanding Community Volunteers; Award the Gertrude Woods Scholarship to outstanding graduating senior each year; Annual recognition for retiring teachers; Sponsor children to attend the special needs handicapped camp each year; Co-sponsor Make A Difference Day with special needs children at coliseum; Sponsor the Houston High School Anchor Club. A new service project is BrainMinders™, teaching brain awareness safety to school children to prevent traumatic brain injuries.

Some of the fundraising projects are: Arts and Crafts, food booths and vendors at Annual Spring Flywheel Festival in April, Wal-Mart matching grant hamburgers cookout, and Fall dinner and auction or raffle during the Annual Fall Flywheel Festival in September.

Past presidents for the Pilot Club of Houston include: Gertrude Woods (2), Ruth Whitt, Mable Cole, Ira Mae Verell (3), Nellie Rose Dendy, Bobbie Nell Pumphrey (3), Mildred Martin, Olivia Rhodes (2), Mabelene Easley (2), Lorene Huffman, Esterlene McKnight, Mary Virginia Baker, Kay Y. Griffin (2), Jane Bowles (2), Mary Davis (3), Jonnie Weaver, Betty H. Brown, Rosie Mabry, Dorajean Sanderson (2), Leona Jerden, Kathy Davis, Laura Bray (3), Linda Young, Bobbie Dulaney and Stacey Curry.

The home of the William D. Sykes Post No. 7149 of the Veterans of Foreign Wars, Houston, MS.

Jane Bowles, Jonnie Weaver and Esterlene McKnight at work on a project for the Pilot Club of Houston, 1983.

Delphian Club, 1991. Seated, L-R: Marge Alexander, Frances Priest, Catherine Simpson, Elizabeth Ellard, Kathrine Roebuck, Carmen Ball, Marge Alford, Tommie Davis and Nig Patch. Standing L-R: Jeanette Estes, Ann Love, ?, Charlotte McQuary, Maxine Murphree, Harriet Pearson, Elizabeth Ellard and Ruby Horn.

Currently known as the Trace Regional Hospital Auxilliary, pictured here are today's members, representing thousands of hours of volunteer service to the local hospital, its staff and patients.

Organized in 1978 as the Houston Medical Center Volunteers, two charter members still active today as "Pink Ladies" are Inez Vanlandingham (left) and Florence Colburn.

CHUQUATONCHEE CHAPTER
NATIONAL SOCIETY OF THE
DAUGHTERS OF THE AMERICAN REVOLUTION
ORGANIZED NOVEMBER 1975

MSSDAR Officers Virginia Brickell, Dell Scoper, Ann Maxwell and Emma Crisler with Elizabeth Crosthwait, Regent, and Marion Fox, Registrar, at the dedication of the Marker at Prospect United Methodist Church, May 7, 2000.

Chuquatonchee Chapter Charter Members at the Chapter 25th Anniversary Celebration: Frances Edens, Earline Gregory, Betty Atkinson and Ann Miskelly.

1998 MSSDAR Outstanding Junior Member Elizabeth Fox Crosthwait and 2001 MSSDAR Outstanding Junior Member Sara Martin Fox page at the 2002 State Conference.

REGENTS

Carolyn Stickerod Snyder	1975-1977
Sarah Tillman Blissard	1977-1979
Mary Ruth Johnson Harrington	1979-1981
Earline McCombs Gregory	1981-1983
Betty Scott Atkinson	1983-1985
Martha Estes Gordon	1985-1987
Roselyn Moore Farr	1987-1989
Elaine Nanny Spencer	1989-1991
Lois Ann Goddard Colbert	1991-1993
Roselyn Moore Farr	1993-1995
Marion Miller Fox	1995-1998
Elizabeth Fox Crosthwait	1998-2002

Charter Members of the Horse Nation Society of the Children of the American Revolution at the 1996 Organizing ceremony at the Houston First Methodist Church. Front row from left: Hillary Horn, Paige Horn, Melissa Dexter, Kaitlyn Caroline Sullivan, Curtis Lehr, John Andrew Brewer, Jordan Ernest, Laura Catherine Horn. Second row from left: Elizabeth Crosthwait, Organizing Senior President, Gray Crosthwait, Robert Earnest, Jeanna Dexter, Blair Norman, Mary Kansas Sullivan, Stacey Earnest, Josh Earnest, Richard Earnest. Back row from left: Sheldon Cole Brewer and his Dad, Colbert Lehr and his Mom, Anna Kathryn Colbert and her Dad, Marion Fox.

SCHOOLS OF CHICKASAW COUNTY

Liberty Hill School at Holladay, MS, about 1893. Children include Holladays, Waldrops, Atkinsons, Phillips, Alexanders, Craigs, Griffins, Turmans, Kennedys, McIntoshes and Johnsons.

Center Hill School, circa 1894. Front row, 7th and 8th from left: Eleanor and Era Chenault.

Miss. Normal College in Houston 1899-1900. Professor H.B. Abernethy in front of tree at center. The building burned in 1904.

Martin School in the woods, Thorn, MS. Includes Henry Duncan, Lonnie Duncan, Oma Blissard, Clytee Blissard, Pecolia Bailey, Wilton Johnston, Maylene Barnett, Walton Blissard, Ulmer Blissard, John Duncan, Gaston Duncan, Clint Moore, Jimmy Jackson Martin, Vardaman Moore, Noel Alford, Annie Martin, Pearl Duncan, Lola Evans and Kathleen Roebuck.

Mississippi Normal College, 1903. Back row, far right Evelyn Sligh (Terry); next row, 6th and 7th from left Zilda E. Gladney (Mitchell) and Clytee Evans. Next row, 2nd from left is Fannie T. Hightower, last two on far right Annie Davis Matthews and Karenza Davis Gelfoy. Boy on far left is ? Whitmore; center is Will ? and on right is Osma Baird. Teacher is Mr. Collins.

Midway School, circa 1908, located 1 mile NW of Bethel Church. Later moved to Sonora Community near Prospect. Moved still later across from Durell Gann home on Hwy. 389. Consolidated about 1927.

Houston Public School, 1908

Okolona School children-date unknown. First row, L-R: Sidney Glass, Nettie Cox, Lorane McKinley, ? Hopkins, Gertrude Jones, Marian Glass, Annie Lou Dean, Velma Reeder, Gladys Sadler. Second row L-R: Leva Spencer, Annie Mae Gregory, ?, Harriett Hendricks, May McGehee, Faye Taylor, Louise Marable, Marian King, Jennie Harris, Lula Mae Shell-teacher. Third L-R: Jack Sansom, Herman Ridly, Joe Beaty, Charlie McGehee, Willie B. Huley, Tonquin Stovall, Brandon Green.

Hickory Ridge School. 1-Teacher Modess Moffit, 2-Herman Walters, 3-Lannie McLaughlin Wooldridge, 4-Orene Clark, 5-Eunice Walters Alford, 6-Laura Turman, 7-Lethia Turman ?, 8-Theodore McClure, 9-Rad Morphis, 10-Wayne Mooneyham, 11-Walter McClure, 12-J.T. Clark, 13-Sybil Pettit, 14-Vannie Clark, 15-Opion Mooneyham, 16-Estell Morphis, 17-Mabel Sumner, 18-Laura Turman, 19-Ethel McClure, 20-Mack Morphis, 21-Lavonne Mooneyham, 22-Mildred McLaughlin, 23-Ruth Hunter Clark, 24-Lethia Turman ?, 26-28 are Turman boys, 29-Haskell McLaughlin and 30 is another Turman boy.

Hickory Ridge School, year unknown. Second from right on back row is Effie Johnson Reeves. Built in the 1800s, the school was located on Blissard property in the Thorn area.

Buena Vista School: Second row, 5th boy from left (in white shirt and tie) is Richard (Dick) Nelson, born Dec. 24, 1901; to his left is Joe L. Nelson, born Oct. 18, 1906.

Enon School 1910. Nellie Rose Marion, teacher; Annie L. Steven Montgomery, assistant.

Columbus Doss Lowry, student at Mississippi A & M, 1911-12.

Bluff Springs School, 1912. Top row, all L-R: Robert Farr, ?, Chess Porter, Nettie Trammel, Clifton Hollingsworth, ?, Tommy Louis Farr, ?, ?, ?. Second: Chess Porter, Nell Porter, Annie Lou Canipe, App Porter, ?, Sybil Farr, ?, Lizzie Farr, ?. Third: Dewitt Trammel, Dwight Martin, ?, Henry Nabors, ?, Armstrong Farr, ?, ?, ?, ?, Florence Nabors. Fourth row: Dewitt Martin, Ola Martin, Grady Martin, Earlene Martin, ?, Evans Farr, Herbert Farr, ?, ?, Robert Nabors, Irene Canipe, ?, Lillie Bell Porter, ?.

Macedonia School, 1915. Genna Lou Murphy and Laudie Sanders teachers.

Center Hill School, circa 1915. Back row, all L-R: Lemuel Davis, Bessie Seay, Autry Davis, Arti Bishop, Leon Neal, Cary Seay, ?. Second row: Alma Turman, ?, Grace Seay, Grace Neal, Willie Turman. Third row: Frances Turman, Tolt Turman, Eunice Chenault, Estelle Seay, Jewell Turman, Susie Mae Neal, Mae Chenault, Loraine Turman. Bottom row: Noel Davis, Orial (Buck) Turman, S.F. Carter, Everett Turman and Robert Neal.

Martin School, Thorn, MS, 1915-16. L-R, first row: Lucas Higginbotham, Roy Evans, Lynn Ferguson, Chester Stroup, Fred Barnett, Roy Chop, Jim Martin, Lonnie Duncan, Jack Barnett, Cecil Lovelace, Lathare Roebuck, Virdie Griffin, Maylene Nabors, Corrine Anderson, Rosie Griffin. Second row: Leola Griffin, Emma Griffin, Addie Evans, Eunice Alford, Ida Alford, Claire Hulston, Ann Anderson, Dorothy Griffin, Grace Griffin, Florence Anderson, Lucille White, Oma Stroup, Pecolia Duncan, Claire Mae Kellum, Smith Evans. Third row: Auvern Ferguson, Henry Duncan, Vannie Griffin, Addie Barnett, Emma Duncan, Lola Evans, Evvie White, Effie Higginbotham, Kelly Moore, Lorena Naron, Viola Barnett and teacher Theresa Blissard White and Dewitt Blissard. Fourth row: Annie Mae Hightower, Jimmie Kellum, Chess Griffin, Vardaman Moore, Jack Evans, Boyd Griffin, Guin Ferguson, Howard Ke?, Roy Anderson, Gaston Duncan, Meredith Huffman-teacher. Fifth row: Lillian Higginbotham, Lula White, Burren Higginbotham, Lilly Bell Griffin, Jessie Moore, Wilburn Naron, Idell White and Gertie Higginbotham.

Houston High School class of 1917. Front row L-R: Zelma Wells, Ruby Lee Ford, Gladys Wilkerson, May Lorene Ford, Tessie Cook. Standing L-R: Ben Woods, Dannie Gordon, Bryan Smith, Bertha May Buchanan, Everett Jeans, Hugh Young West, Evans Riley, Gertrude Reid, Walterene Beasley.

Houston High School, photo made 1918. School building utilized from 1906-1926.

Houston School class picture, around 1920. Bottom L-R: Regina Williams, Ruth Jones, Annabelle ?, Gladys Williams, Frances Hill, Joe M. Ruff, Lou Harley, Pinky Smith, Ralph Ward, Cedric Dendy. Second L-R: Marianne Reid, Walterine Wilkinson, Minnie A. Tabb, Thelma Terry, Elizabeth Huddleston, Sadie Carter, Eunice Chenault, Linnie Pearson, Jewel White. Third L-R: ? Flemmings, Gladys Baird, Margaret Sanders, Eudel Berry, Minnie Alford, Myrtle Byars. Fourth L-R: Lockhart Childress, Lorette (Bill) Baird, Jim Hugh Tabb, Morris Fuller?, Reuben Davis. Fifth L-R: Wilburn Guest, Bob Chenault, Jeff Rish, Malcolm Davis, Roger Brannon, Paul Wright, Dunbar Brand. Top L-R: Speed Bays?, Professor L.B. Reid, Wilburn Davis, Hampton Jones.

Woodland School, as it appeared on November 15, 1920. Constructed shortly before 1920 at a cost of $7,000.00. A.J. Harrington, Jr. served as principal in the 1920s.

Left: Mantee High School, 1923

Chickasaw County AHS, 1924. Third from left is Maie Weed.

Van Vleet Consolidated School, Van Vleet, MS, 1924. Includes families such as Wilson, Peden, Dyer, Marion.

Buena Vista Agricultural High School, 1923-24. First row fourth from left is Herman McCullough; fourth row second from left is Madge Chrestman McCullough; parents of Derwood McCullough.

Houston High School Freshman Class of 1924. Boys from the left: Malcolm Davis, Earnest Glover, Harold Sigler, Prof. L.B. Reid, Henry Guest, Laurett Baird, Frank Gilliam, Lemuel Dossett, Hugh McBride, Russell Wright. Girls top row: Josie Harrington, Norma Williams, Lottie Nabors, Louise Marion, France Helms. Girls bottom row: Estelle McKinney, Grace McWhorter, Virginia Lyles, Kate Thomas, Bonnie Henley, Wilma Baird, Elizabeth Knox, Elease Davis.

Houston School, 1924, 7th grade. Bottom L-R: Cora Shields, Sarah L. Champion, Lucille Austin, Bill Berry, ? McKithin, ?, Clytee Bryant. Seated on left Augustus (Gus) Davis. Second row: Paul Neal, Rapael Arnette, Sam Rish, Lucille Weaver, Mary Seay, ?, Tessie Davis. Third row: Wesley Kyle, Noel Gilliam, Annie ?, Ruth ?, Ruth Atkinson, ?, Josie Harrington. Fourth row: James House, Martha L. Tabb, Maxine Randle, Mary Ruth Johnson, Mary Lacey. Fifth row: Irvin Carlisle, Waldo Kyle, ?, Prof. L.B. Reid, Vester Page, J.R. Priest, Jr., William Reid and James Claude Hightower.

Houston High Senior Class, 1925. Top Row from left is Hamp Jones and Jim Hugh Tabb.

Houlka High School, Freshman Class of 1926-27.

Chickasaw County Agricultural High School Senior Class, 1927-28, Buena Vista, MS. Back row L-R: Dulin 'Guber' Lancaster; Ruby Pearl 'Pearlie' Ellis, Jim 'Bad Jim' Brand, Evelyn 'Boots' Nettles, Miss Susie Williams (class sponsor); Robert 'Bob' Bost; Myrtle 'Full Back' Ginn, William 'Reverend' Cox; Lois Neal, Shelton 'Shortie' Brand. Front row L-R: Rostella 'Cotton' Newell; Richard 'Dick' Bean, Jr., Alyene 'Peach' Lowery; Jimmie 'Hot Papa' Lindsay; Maynette 'Nett' Bowen, Alvis 'Runt' Cook; Celeste 'Less' Ross and Howard 'Hussie' Goodwin.

Pearsall School, approx. 1927. Front L-R: Travis, Alvin and Gladys Nolan, Ruby Lee Verell, Meda and Ireda Wilson, Orene Doss, Margaret Gordon, Bennie Mae O'Barr, D.F. Wilson, Milton Shelton. Second L-R: Ralph Woodruff, Leonard and Durell Gann, T.J. Martin, Emmitt Houser, Judie O'Barr, Lessie Wilson, Bernice Verell, Ona Houser, Velma Woodruff, Gladys Gordon, Allene Doss, Vida O'Barr, Doris Woodruff, Beatrice Verell. Third L-R: ? Saxon, Irma Woodruff, Earnest Pumphrey, Mr. Bob Shelton, Christine Gordon, Lucille Woodruff, Carl Gordon, Mrs. Mary Austin, Boyd Criddle, Elkin Woodruff, Lula Holleman, Lesbie Wilson, Mildred Woodruff, Mable O'Barr.

Fourth grade of Houston School, year unknown. Guy Smith is far left, top row.

Okolona Seniors, 1928. First L-R: Ed Russell Burkett, Marie Louise Fitzgerald, Drew Milstead, Addie Harris, Joseph Johnson, Paula Cohen, Red Andrews, Neomi White, Earl Stawood, Sara George Sanders, Archie Haley, Edith Morgan, Richard King, Helen Johnson. Back row L-R: Lucile Milstead, Armon Wicks, Alice Hodges, Dewitt Gay, Mable Bacon, Sam Lloyd, Mary Sykes Cunningham, Leynne Wiygal, John Quinn, Maude Hill, Lonick Haley, Emma Schwill.

Miss Zelda Dye and her pupils at Pyland. Included are members of the McCluney, Kendall, Sykes, Henry, Hutchison, Thomas, Chapman, Philpot, Norris, Wilson, Gentry, Hensley and Holiday families.

Houston's Second Grade Class, circa 1910. Third from right, bottom row is Mary Hickman. Classmates would have included Walter E. Scott, Jr. and Catherine Shell Davis.

Okolona High School Seniors, 1930-31. Seated L-R: Thomas McConnell, Cora Gates Richardson, Bill Tyson, Sarah Andrews, Tom Grauer, Katherine Jones, William Abernethy, Annie Bearden. Second row L-R: Tony Stanford, Frances Guin, Hazel Blaylock, Betty Davenport, Prest Baskin, Margorie Jones, Earline Andrews, Imogene Rowe, Dorothy Bell. Back row L-R: Edwin Wilson, Shelby Wilson, Miss Henry (sponsor), Manley Gregory, Cora Mae Johnson, Josephine Richardson, Robert Farned, Ellis Latimer.

Houston High School Sophomore Class of 1930-31. Girl on second row in dark dress with white collar is Odean Putnam.

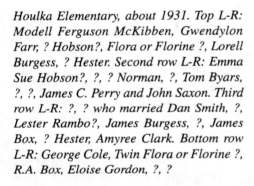

Houlka Elementary, about 1931. Top L-R: Modell Ferguson McKibben, Gwendylon Farr, ? Hobson?, Flora or Florine ?, Lorell Burgess, ? Hester. Second row L-R: Emma Sue Hobson?, ?, ? Norman, ?, Tom Byars, ?, ?, James C. Perry and John Saxon. Third row L-R: ?, ? who married Dan Smith, ?, Lester Rambo?, James Burgess, ?, James Box, ? Hester, Amyree Clark. Bottom row L-R: George Cole, Twin Flora or Florine ?, R.A. Box, Eloise Gordon, ?, ?

Houston High School class of 1931.

Van Vleet Senior Class, 1932-33. Back row, all L-R: John Collins, Teacher; Neely Atkinson, Hugh Collins, Teacher; Grace Wilson (Beaty-Eaton), Benjamin Carter, Rev. H.M.Collins, Principal. Front: Nettie S. Peden (Ray), Annie Lee Collins (Scott), Preston Carter, Jr., Mary Virginia Baker, Winifred Walters (Marion).

Program	Class Roll	
THEME: THE COMMUNITY AND EDUCATION		

Program	Class Roll	
Processional: "March of the Noble" ....Keats	Willie Maude Baird	Sydnette Kimball
Quartette: "In the Luxembourg Gardens" ...Riegger	Virginia Grace Blissard	Rosa Jeanette McIntosh
Frances Byars, Anna Ruth Byars,	Paul Dulaney Bray	Frances Louise Medlin
Graham Golson and Robert Atkinson	Mary Frances Byars	Walker Overall
What the Town Owes the School	Thomas Henry Dalton	Doris H. Paden
Francs Louise Medlin, Salutatorian	David Evans Davis	Dora Odean Putnam
Piano Solo: "Valse Caprice" .... Newland	W.D. Garner	James Bowie Reid
Grace Philpot	Graham E. Golson	Mavolyn Sanderson
Education for Service, for Leisure, and for Living	Mary Lou Harrington	Nellie Ruth Seay
Graham Golson, Class Orator	Margaret Lesbia Hill	James Dugan Shell
Vocal Solo: "My Creed" ....Garrett	Jack Thompson Holloman	Martha Eileen Stubblefield
Miss Maude Mabry	Lucille Holliday	Emma Louise Thompson
Address .... Hon. Fred M. Belk	John J. Huffman	Robert Verell
Delivery of Diplomas.		
What the School Owes the Town		
Sydnette Kimball, Valedictorian		
Class Song: "Faith in the Future" ....Lord		
Recessional		

Graduation program and class roll for the class of 1933, Houston High School.

Houlka School bus drivers in the early 1930s when drivers had to buy their own buses. L-R: Roscoe Shirley, Jody Lester, Furman Harris, Fred James, Walter Lancaster, Joe L. Davis and janitor, Dexter Daniel.

151

Anchor School, before 1939. Front L-R: Gladys Knox, Velma Lancaster, Clara Mae Hill, Emma Dean Nichols, Sidnett Dendy. Second row L-R: Mrs. Idell Scarbrough, Norman Hill, Rufus W. Nichols, Winston (Shorty) Hampton. Third row L-R: Edward Hill, Daniel Louis Howell. Fourth row L-R: Robert Griffin, Scott Dendy, Richard Dendy, Garland Dendy, Willis Griffin, Arnold Howell and Curtis Owen Hampton.

One of the early classes of nurses from the Houston Hospital, about 1935-36. Third from left is Eva Collins Tabb, (secretary to Dr. Van Philpot, Sr. and not a nurse) and sixth from left, back row, is Nellie Rose Harwood Dendy.

Thorn School at second school building. Back row standing L-R: Charles Langley, Patsy Moore, Madge Moore, Oma Ruth McGee, Eva Jean Wooldridge, Sue Moss ?, Wayne Moss, Alice Moss, Paul Ray Moss. Middle row L-R: Joyce Kimbrough, ?, Evelyn Moore, ?, Hurley Higginbotham. Front L-R ?, Kenneth Moore, Douglas Anderson, ?, Dan Langley, Clifton Moore, Billy Joe Langley, Gerald Johnson, Sidney G. Barnett.

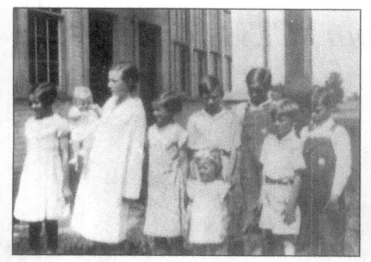

Left: Martin School house, Thorn, MS, 1936. L-R: Virginia Duncan, Troy Griffin held by Maudin Cook, Helen Cook, Herman Cook, Betty Jean Cook in front of Herman, Billy Joe Cook and Floyd Cook.

Right: The old school building at Hohenlinden, 1937.

Okolona High School, Class of 1939. Top row from left: Clarence McLanahan, Betty Sue Reifers, Luther Jolly, Martha Polk, A.M. Kidd, Nellie Mae Culp and Hal Holloway. Second row from bottom, from left: James E. McCain, Anne McGehee, Mildred Duncan, Sara Carlile, Charles Martin and J.C. Stone. Left of piccture, top to bottom: James Rappe, Blance Busby, A.W. James (superintendent) and Eva Lowell. Right of picture, top to bottom: Miriam Arnold, William Duncan, Frances Bailey (sponsor) and Elizabeth Fitzgerald. Bottom row from left: Charles Jolly, Nancy Kathryn Hodges, Arthur Blaylock, Alice Hyatt McDuffie, Herbert Sullivan, Olivia Lowell and Foy Dismukes.

HOULKA HIGH SCHOOL, CLASS OF 1939

As of April 1, 2002, eight of the Class of 1939 are living. Other pictures of this class may be found on Burt-McKee family pages and perhaps others.

Graduation Sunday, April 23...Steps of the old Baptist Church. Left side: James Seay Perry, Curtis Roncyl Young. Right side: Charles Delane Easley, Leland Brown Norman. Bottom step: Maralee Kirby, Elouise Gordon, Mascot Mike Smith, Sarah Elizabeth Norman, Jimmie Kimbrough. Second step: Emma Sue Hobson, Ruth Holladay, Virginia Louise Bullard, Laverne Harwood, Lorell Burgess. Foyer row one: William Arthur White, Hulet Leon Owen, James Augustus Burt, Jr., Thomas Winter Roberts. Foyer row two: John Wesley Holladay, Maurice Durell Thompson, Walter Saxon McGee, Milton Robert Shelton.

Reunion 1973, School Cafeteria. Front, seated: Burgess (McNatt)l Hobson (Young); Bullard (Norman); Harwood (Cain). Middle standing: Gordon (Graves); Kirby (Boydston); Kimbrough (Malone). Back: Young, Easley, Burt, Perry, Shelton, McGee.

Reunion 1985, Burt home: Row one: Kirby (Boydston); Bullard (Norman); Gordon (Graves); Harwood (Cain). Row two: Young, Burt, Easley, McGee, Shelton, Holladay. Row three: Roberts, Thompson, Austin.

Fiftieth Reunion, 1989, Burt home. Front: Thompson, Burt; Bullard (Norman); Kimbrough (Malone); Gordon (Graves); Burgess (McNatt). Second: White; Austin; Perry; Shelton; Harwood (Cain); Easley; Holladay.

Reunion 1990, Easley home. Front: Gordon (Graves); Kirby (Boydston); Kimbrough (Malone); Bullard (Norman); Burgess (McNatt). Back: Holladay, Burt, Easley, Austin, McGee, Thompson.

Reunion 1995, Burt home. Front: Austin, Burt, Thompson. Back: McGee; Harwood (Cain); Bullard (Norman); Gordon (Graves); Easley.

Sixtieth Reunion, Holliday Terrace, 1999. Easley; Bullard (Norman); Burgess (McNatt); Gordon (Graves); Harwood (Cain); McGee.

Anchor School, probably 1939 or 1940. Front row L-R: Miss Everena Harris Dendy, Charles Hill, Peyton McQuary, Estelle Hill, Wauweese McQuary, Hortense Nichols, Donald Dean Coffin. Second row, L-R: Elizabeth Hampton, LaNelle Lancaster, Melba Dobbs, Gene Dobbs, Paul Dendy, Clifton Hill. Third row L-R: Robert Hill, H.B. Box, Doug Dendy, Naron Lancaster, Henry Box and Rufus Griffin.

Okolona Public School, Okolona, MS. This building was torn down in 1924.

The old Pearsall School building, 1st through 8th grade.

Pyland School, date unknown. Back row l-r: Miss Essie Cockrell, ?, Lillian McDaniel, Shorty Thomas, Loretta Thomas, Shag Lowe, Anna Spencer, Hawkins Kendall, Geneva Norris, Pud Thomas, Miss Zelda Dye. Middle row l-r: Johnnie Earnest, Ruth Ann Hensley, Pat Hutchinson, Dot Lowe, John Buren Kendall, Sonny Philpot, Alice Franklin, ?, Colleen Thomas. Front l-r: Clara Franklin, ?, ?, Hilda Franklin, ?, Nelda Philpot, ?, ?.

Left: State Band Contest in Jackson, 1940. L-R: Buford Woods, Roland Westbrook and Billy Smith of Houston in front of the Edwards Hotel.

Right: Students in Miss Essie Cockrell's "Primer" at Pyland, MS. Seated left, with army cap on is Robert O. (Bob) Kendall, the little girl seated on the right is Shirley Hawkins Lowry. Middle child is James Sykes?. John Sykes may be the boy standing on left.

Okolona High School, built in the late 1920s.

Pleasant Grove School, Thorn, MS. L-R: Mary Ruth Blissard, Clarice Wooldridge, Lorena Doss, Annie Laurice Langley, Virginia Doss, Christine McGee.

Woodland School class picture, year not certain. Third from left, bottom row is Leon Martin.

Houston High School Band, 1940-41. First row: Dewells Barton (director), Jimmye Doss, Agnes Page, George Armstrong, Buford Woods, Bennett Blanton, Juanice Harrington, Joann Lowry, Jane Evans Lowry, Eloise Ford, Van Philpot, Marjorie Philpot. Second row: Linda McCluney (majorette), Frances Beasley, T.A. Bryant, Jack Reed, Buddy Stewart, Floyd Seay, Dorothy Jean Rhodes, Roy Harmon, Rosemary Lowry, Bill Smith, J.I. Lowry, Sid Bowles. Third row: John White, Jean Berry, Joe Rhodes, Felix Rutledge, Sonny Page, C.D. Bouchillon, Jack Barrett, John Walker Ray, Kimball Brown. Fourth row: Rubel Burgess, Alvin Westbrook, ?, Lee Burgess, Gene Shotts, Dera Sigler, Pete Nichols, ?, Rose Chandler, Joe Franklin, Russell Putman, Frank Brand, (Drum Major), Sam Tom Scott, Majorettes Frances Harrington on left, LaVerne Wray on right.

Houston High School, Class of 1941

Pleasant Grove School, Thorn, MS, 1942-43. L-R: Billy Carlisle, John Hall, Rubye Lee Barnett, Laverle Wooldridge, Loretta Langley, Faye Clark, Sue Moss.

Pleasant Grove School, Thorn, 5th Grade, 1942-43. L-R: Travis Williams, Darricott Mooneyham, Gordon Huffman, Imogene Higginbotham, Etoyle ?, Bobbie Nell Kellum, Shirlene McGee.

Pleasant Grove School, Thorn, 3rd grade, 1942-43. L-R: Gene Hall, Gearld Morris James, Colleen Kellum, Sarah Moore, Bobbie Jean Stroup and Marcell McGee. Second row L-R: Owen Langley, Paul Bray, Ruth Wooldridge, Martha Frances Mahan, Aline Wright, Mara Anna Turman and Gracie Mae McGee.

The Houston High School Class of 1944. L-R: Boyce Roebuck, Marvin Simms, Tom Holder, Mr. S.F. Smith (Superintendent), Mary Frances Collins, Marvin Dendy, Jenoise McCay, Virginia Hastings, Ruth Ray, Sid Bowles, Margaret Mixon, Louise Naron, Clayton Stewart, Allie Mae Scruggs, Mary Evelyn Helms, Kathleen Bounds, Estelle Heair, Jimmye Doss, Peggy Luke, Grace Gann, Juanice Neal, Eunice House, Kimball Brown, Jane Lowrey, Leon Foster, Sarah Vancleave, Zora Lee Bean, Lucy Morgan, Nancy Chenault, Laverne Brown, Clifton Rhodes.

Left: Enon School about 1944: Front: Grace Griffin. Second row L-R: Laverne Griffin Walters, Rene Duncan (Finn). Third L-R: Jennie Lee Huffstatler, Francis Huffstatler, Dorothy Branch (Thomas). Back L-R: Bud Branch and Billy Couch.

Right: Vic Metts, high school coach, promoted to superintendent of the Houston public school system in February 1946, succeeding S.F. Smith.

Houston High School, Class of 1946.

Okolona High School, Senior Class of 1946.

Houlka High School Class of 1947 the day of graduation. First row L-R: Dale Brown, Doris McKnight Shelton, Reba F. Anderson, Mable Zachary Murphree, Martha A. Brown Farish and Ruby Andrews Moses. Second row L-R: Jean Paden Cruse, Betty J. Brock Hamilton, Jane Norman Zachary, Godie Bailey Hardin, Jane Thomas McDonald, Allen Harris, Zula Holley Moceri, Ray Houston, Margaret Collums Sturdivant, Bobbie J. Holladay Laughlin, Bob Graves, Charles Brown, T.J. Roberts, Reginald Henry, Lanelle Tallent Mason, Faye Shirley Bishop and Billy Fate Murphree.

Houston High School, Senior Class of 1947.

Left: Virginia Brand (Pumphrey), daughter of W.A. "Bo" and Minnie Finn Brand in the last year for Egypt High School before students were sent to other schools; 1947-48.

Right: Andrew Jackson (A. J.) Harrington, Jr., Superintendent of Chickasaw County schools from 1948-1952.

SENIOR CLASS 1948

Left: Woodland High School, Class of 1947-48. Front row L-R: Mrs. J.S. Crubaugh, Jewel Gordon, Jimmie Dale Brents, Doris Moore, Althea Scott Brand, Sue Gordon. Back row, L-R: Cedric Walters, Daniel Lewis Howell, M.F. Brents, Henry J. Eaton.

Below: Houston High School Band at the Delta Band Festival, Greenwood, MS, 1948. Front L-R: Louise Lowry, Joynelle Pearson, Lyman Thomas, Archie Miller, Richard Pratt, Darrell Martin, Cecil Threat, Mary E. Hill, Ethel Edwards, Joann Ray. Second row L-R: Drum Major Henry Thompson, Wanda Hollowell, Gary Atkinson, Scottie Alford, Thomas Rowlett, A.J. Gann, Patsy Huskinson, Johnny Wilson, Mary J. Ford, Mr. W.B. Oswalt. Third L-R: David Woods, Francis Naron, Marie Burks, Ella Johnson, Joan Woods, Frankie Weaver, Lynn Fant, Eddie Doss, Leon Harrington, Mary (Nig) Springer. Fourth L-R: Gene Hall, Les Sumner, Robert Shelton, Charlie Miller, Gene Byars, Jack Linn, Sue Hollowell, Sam Gore, Billy B. Hill, Sonny Eurie. Fifth L-R: Hugh McCullough, Billy Beasley, Carl Martin, Paul Dendy, Douglas Dendy, Woodrow Brand, ?, Joyce Bryant, Bobby O'Barr and Lamar Harrington.

Houston High School, Senior Class of 1948. Class members are: Beth Nell Jernigan, Lesbia Clark, Juanita Ford, Annelle McCay, W.V. Metts (Superintendent) Jack Henry Ray, Martha Kate Wimberly, Wesley Baird, Joynelle Pearson, Maxine Lancaster, Virginia Shotts, Lucille Blansett Jones, Darrell Hugh Martin, Mary Alice Moseley, Dan Griffin, Marjorie Holder, Johnnie Dell Langley, Amaline Crawford, Betty Jean Ashby, James Robert Gann, Louise Criddle, Virginia Ann Martin, Lamar Harrington, Bobby Barrett, Martha Smith, Melba Glenn Marion, J.C. Weaver, Jane Hodges, Ruth Woodruff, Marilyn Faye Henry, V.L. Weaver and Richard Platt. Not pictured is Mrs. L.B. Reid, Sponsor.

Houston High School, Class of 1949. Class members are: Billy Gene Sykes, Maxine Smith, Pascal Barron, Geralene Oswalt, Mr. W.V. Metts (Superintendent), Peggy Sue Garrett, Joyce Abernethy, Charles Rhodes, Leamond Alford, Bobby O'Barr, Harley Langley, Lottie Mae Blansett, Imogene Oswalt, Joann Ray, Allene Mitchell, Sue Cox, Doyle Wooldridge, Roselyn Moore, Ethel Edwards, Leslie Sumner, Charles Miller, Hugh McCullough, Henry Thompson, Mary Kathryn Salmon, Dwight Griffin, Creely Neal Myatt, Grace Kellum, Harold Craig, Mary Roane Hill, Frances Stone, Emogene Clements, Louise Turman, Herbert Miller, Monela Moore, A.E. Davis Jr., Mary Ella Springer, Norma Chenault and Joyce Bryant. Not pictured is Mrs. L.B. Reid, Sponsor.

Houston High School, Class of 1950. Class members are: Cecil F. Thweatt, Nathalene Lowrey, Minnie Pearl Lancaster, Maxine Foster, D.L. Harrington, W.V. Metts (Superintendent), Kent Hightower, Joann Woods, Faye Farr, James Robert Neal, A.J. Gann Jr., Dorothy Lowe, Loyd Griffin, Thomas Rowlett, Jo Kirkpatrick, Robert Charles Kimble, Jack Thompson, Alice Franklin, Frances Naron, Clarence Philpot, David Woods, Etoyle Higginbotham, James Thomas, Gene Hall, Sarah Thompson, Edward Springer, Bobbie Nell Kellum, Douglas Dendy, Elizabeth Thompson, Max Murphree Cole, Omeria Nabors, Everett Day Jr., Frankie Rose Weaver, Maurice Elmo Bounds and Marie Burks. Not pictured is Mrs. L.B. Reid, Sponsor.

Houston High School, Class of 1952. Class members are: Bettie Colbert, Ruth Wooldridge, Virginia Smith, Maurene Clark, Clytee Brock, Selma Smith, Robert Shelton, Miriam Day, Rex Warnick, Mr. W.V. Metts (Superintendent), Larry Carter, Virginia Nabors, Jack Linn, Gloria Bowman, Joan Mixon, Charles Briscoe Jr., Nellie Robertson, Joyce Townley, Loudene Criddle, Mamie Colbert, William Moore, David Hill, Billy Sanders, Grace Johns, Robinette Gann, Jimmy Lancaster, Charles Henry, James Doss, Martha Brand, Sue Hollowell, Helen Baird, Sarah Moore, Bert Hill, Dorothy Atwell, Margaret Nelson, Lovey McCown, Clara Franklin, Bobby Yarborough, Lester Cheatham, Bobby Nabors, Louise Horn, Ruby Robertson, Betty Farr, Robbie Foster, Juanita Chenault, June Moore, Mary Rhodes, Gary Atkinson and Lawrence Smith Jr.

Houston High School, Class of 1954. Class members are: Auzie Myatt, Hugh Vickery, Lanelle Garner, James Blue, Mr. W.V. Metts (Superintendent), Mrs. W.V. Metts (Sponsor), Gene Byars, Margaret Kyle, Max Kimbrough Jr., Bobby Dendy, Virginia Rish, Billy Thomas, Durwanda Dendy, Simuel Naron, Nancy Nelson, Waymon Russell, Peggy Foster, Gene Griggs, Jeanine Turner, Garland Colbert, Ruby Doss, Don Livingston, Jimmy Gore, Ivonna Young, Jahu Blissard, Naomi Smith, Fred Wilson, Rachel McGee, David Naron, Shirley Huffman, Allan Holliday, Donald Harrington, Jo Ann Briscoe, Bryan Parchman, Joan Davis, John Ford, Louise Hamby, Arden Ellise, Christine Porter, Nyra Nichols, Scottie Allen, Gwendolyn Pearson, Billy White, Neta Dexter and Darrel Griffin.

Woodland High School, Class of 1954, senior trip to Florida. L-R: Charlotte McQuary (Sponsor), Glenda Faye Nichols, Eloise Whitt, Betty Joann Hill, Mildred Bullard, Etoile Faulkner, Bob Wofford, Jerry Dean Smith, Doyle McQuary (Sponsor), Martha Rose Lancaster, Mary Ella Jennings, Bertha Mae Martin, Roy Hill, William Clark, Daniel Dendy, Glen Vance.

L-R: Morris, Herbert, Christine and Cecil Williams at the Houlka School, September 1954.

Earlene Peden, Houston High School history teacher for many years.

Mrs. Sam Goza (or "Miss Felton") at a Jr.-Sr. Banquet, 1956.

Forrest Byars with Superintendent W.V. (Vic) and Mrs. Marianne Metts at Jr.-Sr. Banquet in 1956.

Jr.-Sr. Banquet at the old Community Center, 1955 or 1956. Foreground Dot Gann Wilson, Adolph Davis, Minnie J. Beaty Hill, Jo Ann Clark Herrod.

Scene from the 1957 Houston High School senior play: L-R seated or kneeling: Bess Pearson, Barbara Bivens, Jimmy Nabors, Robert Goza, Randle Russell and Jeannette Park. Standing L-R: Forrest Byars, Mary Lee Goode, Dewayne Griffin, Mary C. Martin, Gordon Pettit, Carolyn Ray, Marion Russell, DeArmon Vance, Betty Blair, Louis Vescova and Elizabeth Ware.

Houston High School, Class of 1957. Front L-R: Mary Catherine Martin, Louis Vescova, Lucy Westbrook, Jimmy Nabors, Marion Russell, Betty Blair, Forrest Byars, Ruth Ann Higginbotham, Linda Kimble, Rex Sanderson, Jeannette Park. Second L-R: Betty Smith, Doris Strawhorn, Elizabeth Ware, Jimmy Knox, Bobby Miller, Bess Pearson, Clara Powell Simpson, Lucille Cooper, Mary Lee Goode, Charlene Knox, Helen Gann. Third L-R: DeArmon Vance, Bill Sisk, Jerry Cox, Betty Dendy, Carolyn Ray, Rose Smith, Jack Wilson, Barbara Bivens, Robert Goza. Fourth L-R: Tommy Smith, Howard Fleming, Thomas Guest, Alva Ray McCorkle, Charles Neal, Gordon Pettit, Bobby Mixon, Randle Russell, Clyde Ward and Shirley Hawkins.

The Houston High School, Class of 1958. Top row from left: Jerry Max Griffin, Peggy Dobbs, Dan Langley, Barbara Ware, George Taylor, Mr. W.V. Metts (Superintendent), Thomas Edward Smith Jr., Mary Jean Sykes, John R. Simpson, Rebecca Westbrook and Bobby Kilgore. Second row: Reba Chapman, Charles Park, Barbara Mae Bentz, Thomas Wayne Colbert, Sara Ann Miller, Calvin Vanlandingham, Mamie Franks, Tommy Harrington, Evelyn Gann, David Tennyson and Pegge Rhodes. Third row: James Austin Gann, Louise Funderburk, Virginia Ann Harrington and Martha Ann Patch. Fourth row: Ruth Gambrell, Milton Davis, Joyce Gann, Richard Baird, Paul Foster, Jeanne Eastridge, Lamar Beaty and Virginia Hamby. Fifth row: James Robertson, Frances Shields, Don T. Simpson, Joyce Brock Myatt, Betty Coleman, Charlotte Walters, Lucretia Colbert, Thomas Earl Allen, Sara Elizabeth Langley and Sid Dendy. Bottom row: Julia Faye Shempert, James Robert Criddle, Ann Worden, James Huffman, Lorene Griffin, Patsy Bivens, Jimmy Roberson, Sara Love Holliday, Tommy Baird and Peggy Hawkins. Not pictured is Mrs. W.V. Metts, Sponsor.

The Houston High School, Class of 1961.

Mrs. Wallace Norman's Kindergarten Class of 1966-67. Top row, L-R: Lesa Harrington, Ramona Thomas, Lauren Norman, Kay Carnathan, Pipa Fortner, Ellen Bowles, Kathy Thomas and Cammy Nichols. Bottom row, L-R: Brad Smith, Kelly Harrell, Randy Russell, Eddie Griffin, Hugh Meek, Jim Hood, Kevin Ramage and Michael House.

Mamie Rogers' Child Care Center, Okolona, MS, 1967. Front L-R: Maggie Sumner, Joey Criddle, Donna Sumner, Sammy Henderson, George Dallas, Jim Anderson and John Anderson. Second row: Lori Duke, Billy Henderson, Rogers Criddle, Tim Sullivan, Jr. Henderson, Garland Smith, Paula Ward, Brenda Corley, David McDonald. Back row, L-R: Lottie Rogers Corley and Mamie Martin Rogers.

Houlka bus drivers in 1969 when the county bought the buses. L-R: Mildred Burgess, Roy Berry, Ruby Kirkpatrick substituting for her brother, Ike James; Clara Shirley, John White and John Moore.

Chickasaw Academy students, Van Vleet, MS. L-R: Lynn Brock, Buzz Morrow (Coach), Tommy Brock, Bronco Anderson, Bill Walker and Charlie Hollimon.

The 50th reunion of Houlka, MS, Class of 1924. Every senior of this class graduated from college as well. William Clyde Stewart, Sr. is standing at the far left.

Chickasaw Academy, Class of 1980-81. Top row from left: Orlando Borst, Lee McNeel, Rogers Criddle, Neal Lee. Middle row: Katy Lee Anderson, Gary Norman (Headmaster), Cheryl Ross (Sponsor), Allen Bishop. Bottom row: Brenda Corley, Lydia Jolly Howell, Dewitt Moore, Debra Warren.

Jane Smith, wife of Herman Smith, was Houston Public School system's first nurse. She served in this capacity for 21 years.

The pipes were visible in the ceiling of the cafeteria located in the basement of the old Houston High School, but they did not keep students from enjoying this banquet in the late 1950s.

SPORTS

Anchor girl's ball team, 1925. Standing L-R: Josie Gordon (Blue), Tessie Gordon, Olivia Nichols (Vaughn), Lois Griffin (Weaver). Front L-R: Arlene and Ethel McQuary.

Columbus Doss Lowry, member of Mississippi A & M track team, 1911-12.

Howard (Shorty) H. Roberts, son of Mr. and Mrs. T.R. Roberts, was a winning baseball pitcher for the town of Houlka. He later pitched for the Cotton States league for several years.

Houston's baseball team, 1924 state champs, included "Boozie" Sanderson, far left on back row, and Dave Kyle, second from right back row.

Left: From the personal belongings of Jim Reid, a 1933 graduate of HHS comes this picture. Written on the back was "Pick Nobles and his boy(s) at Houston." P.A. Nobles came to Houston circa 1928 and remained until circa 1936. He is credited with making the "Hilltopper" the school mascot. Nobles participated in the formation of the Little Ten Conference; served as its secretary the first year, its president the next year.

From Jim Reid's pictures–on this one was written "Houston team in 1930 to 1932." P.A. "Pick" Nobles was coach.

Chickasaw Indians, Pyland, MS. Front L-R: Sonny Philpot, Grady Spencer, Charles Henry, Billy Gene Sykes, Hollie Kendall, Zeb Philpot. Back L-R: Cedric (Pud) Thomas, Charles Bevils, Hawkins Kendall, Randolph Franklin, Joe Bevils, T.J. Hulsey and James E. (Shorty) Thomas.

Woodland High School basketball team, about 1936. L-R: Hubert Nabors, J.T. McQuary, Russell Brandon, Bill Harkey, Lee McQuary, Wesley Fant, Curtis Nabors and Quitman Fant.

Woodland Boys basketball team, 1938. Back from left: Buck Ball, Claudia Melton, Durrell Harrington, James Robert Pate and Coach Wilburn Griffin. Front from left: Preston Nichols, J.T. McQuary, Oliver Harrington and John Thomas "Tots" Moore.

171

Jack Gregory, Sr. of Okolona played ball for the Univ. of Alabama until he "nearly starved" in the Depression. Later played for Univ. of Chattanooga where he made All American in 1939. He then played for the Cleveland Rams (at that time the Cleveland Browns).

Elbert E. Corley (1920-1988). High school football in Okolona; college at MS State 1940-46; pro-football for Buffalo Bills in 1947 and Baltimore Colts in 1948. Married to Beverly Cramer, they had Melanie, Melinda, Elbert Jr. and Candace.

Thomas Deward "Dude" McCullough, Houlka High School, 1940.

1941 Woodland basketball team, Doyle McQuary, No. 5

Roy Paden Davis, Houston High School football player, about 1942.

Charlotte McCullough McQuary, Holmes Jr. College basketball player, 1944-1946. Inducted into their Hall of Fame in 2000; Houlka High School basketball player for 5 years.

Houston Travelers, semi-pro team, 1947. Front L-R: Red Baine, "Pop" Gates, Paul Baine. Second L-R: Weldon Harrington, Johnny Grace, Rex Harrington, Ralph Brown, MS State player. Third L-R: Harold "Hap" Baine, two MS State players, John Oren Rhodes. Back row, L-R: Dave Kyle and 3 players from MS State.

Woodland basketball team, 1948. First row L-R: Sara Woodruff Dendy, Dorothy F. Hill, Grace Neal, Mary Allen Gann, Sue Gordon Brents, Lula Ward Hill, Ann Wages Dye. Second row L-R: Thomas Streeter, Doris Moore Ledbetter, Elizabeth Hampton Hollingsworth Weaver, Waweene McQuary Kirby, Jean Moore Smith, Barbara Pumphrey Buchannan, Sara Womack ? and J.S. Crubough.

Houlka girls basketball team, 1948-49. L-R: Dorothy Mae Smith, Ann McCullough, Lillie Fay Kirkpatrick, Peggy McCullough, Louise Caldwell, Janice Roberts, Adeline Mason, Anna Ruth Strait, Betty Sue Henry, Betty J. Caldwell, Martha Shelton, Joan Hinton and Maxine Gann. Coach Percy Burt is not pictured.

From the football program of September 24, 1948. All L-R. Bottom: Les Sumners, Zeb Philpot, Billy Peel, Morris Bounds, Paul Dendy, Billy G. Sykes, Harold Craig. Second: Milton Brown, John Scott, James Thomas, Bobby O'Barr, Charlie Miller, Herbert Faulkner, Archie Miller. Top: Carter Gordon, Clarence Philpot, Hugh McCullough, Lamon Alford, Doc Davis, Reginald Nabors and Leon Harrington.

Woodland basketball team, 1948-49. Front L-R: James Davis Doss, Thomas Verell, George Parker. Second L-R: John Woodruff, Billy C. Hill, Hugh Stevenson, Leon Martin. Back L-R: Coach C.C. Mabry, Robert Nabors, Bobby R. Toland, Forrest Wofford, Roy Bullard, Billy Whitt.

Houston High School football team, 1949. Front row, L-R: Zeb Philpot, Billy Peel, Shorty Thomas, Elmo Bounds, Paul Dendy, Jack Thompson and Carl Martin. Second row L-R: Wayne Kimball, Larry Carter, George Easley, Billy Walls, Gus Ashby, Gary Atkinson, Woodrow Brand, Gary Young. Back row L-R: Joe Brigance, Carter Gordon, Watson Scott, Robert Shelton, Evans Thomas, Robert Kimball, Reginald Nabors, Clarence Philpot, Larry Bonds, Bert Hill and Willie Foster.

Houston High School basketball, 1950. Back row L-R: Elizabeth Mitchell, Marcella Alford, Ruth Wooldridge, Joe Brigance, Robinette Gann, Louise Lowry, Margaret Ann Kyle. Second row L-R: Selma Smith, Sue Hollowell, Sarah Moore, Mary John Ford. Front L-R: Bobbie Sue Saxon and Omeria Nabors. Team mates not pictured include Maxine Springer and Iva Jean Brown. This was 'Coach Joe's' first girl's basketball team. The gym was not completed and practice was on a dirt court. Once a week, the team went to Woodland to practice. Mrs. C.D. Lowry bought fabric for uniforms that were sewn by Miss Lucinda Nichols. She used old Egypt School uniforms to go by.

Woodland girls basketball team, 1950 and 1951. From left: Coach Howard L. Ray, Mary Ella Jennings, Dora Woodruff, Bobbie Womack, Eloise Whitt, Martha Rose Lancaster, Bonnie Martin, Hazel Ware, Clara Hill, Rachel Whitt, Margaret Wofford, Mildred Bullard, Josephine Collums and Jean Moore.

Woodland basketball team, 1950-51. Front L-R: Paul Griffin, Jerry Doss, J.D. Walters, Gene Mabry, John R. Woodruff. Second L-R: Donald Clark, Glen Vance, Leon Martin. Back L-R: A.C. Vance, Jimmy Stevenson, Roy Bullard, Johnny Green, Coach Howard L. Ray.

Houston High School football team, 1951-1952. Front L-R: Charles Gordon, Mahlon Gann, Robert Shelton, Zeb Philpot. Second L-R: Bobby Joe Allen, Joe Criddle, Hubert Gann, Bobby Dendy, John Robert Ford, Wm. Chester Moore. Third L-R: Simuel Naron, Adolph Davis, Max Kimbrough, Jr., Eugene Criddle, Billy Scott, Conway Nichols. Fourth L-R: Sammy Lacey, Walter Gann, Billy Joe Rish, Billy Bert Hill, Jack Hill, Sam Blue and Charlie Lee Griffin.

Woodland girls basketball, 1952-53. L-R: Nellie Sue Martin, Charlotte McQuary, Dora Woodruff, Audrey Moore, Dorothy Box, Mildred Box, Joann Smith, Bernice Houser, Martha Rose Lancaster, Bonnie Martin, Clara Fay Hill, Fay Vance, Mildred Bullard and Josephine Collums. Coach Doyle McQuary in front.

Woodland High School, 1951-52. Back row L-R: David Beason, Luther Whitt, Charles Criddle, Roy Bullard, Jimmie Stevinson, Robert Huffman and Mr. Stafford. Front L-R: Glen Vance, Lonnie Whitt, Jerry Doss, Rex Pumphrey, Donald Aron Houser, Joe Wright.

175

Houlka boys basketball team. 1953. L-R: Harry Rye, Ed Harrison, Tommy Chenault, Billy Joe Berry, Merrill Chrestman, Billy Gene Helms, Billy Wayne MaHarrey, Sonny Thomas, Dennis Howell and Jimmy Dee Tutor.

Houston's boxing team, L-R: Bobby Joe Allen, 160#; Deede Harrington, JC president; Lyman Thomas-170#; Tony Sepulveda, trainer; Hinton Shempert-125#; James Pounders, chairman of boxing committee; Jack Wilson-108# and Ralph Thomas-112#.

Boxing coach Tony Sepulveda with trainer Danny Kay Thomas; boxers L-R: Bobby Mooneyham, 127 lbs.; Douglas Watson, 118 lbs.; Tommy Harrington, 147 lbs.; and Jimmy Parker, 127 lbs.

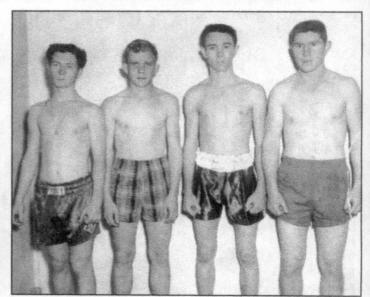

More of Coach Tony Sepulveda's "fighters." L-R: Danny Kay Thomas, Joe Nabors, Bob Chapman and Red Flemings.

John Simpson of Houston is driven down by his opponent at the Golden Gloves bout in Jackson. Referee was Rocky Marciano, retired undefeated world heavyweight champion. Reporter who covered event said Rocky was "kept busy untangling the enthusiastic youngsters."

Flavious "Red" Alford, University of Mississippi; later the much admired "Coach Alford" at Houston High School.

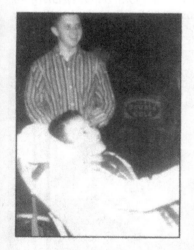

Left: Mackie Weaver broke his leg in a football game in the 1957-58 season. He was taken to the rest of the games that year via ambulance. Shown here with Bobby (Peewee) Kilgore.

Houston High School basketball team, coach and managers, circa 1955-56. From the top and L-R: Coach Joe Brigance, Mamie Franks, Rose Smith, Patty Jo Lowry, Clara Powell Simpson, Lib Harrington, Betty Blair, Sara Ann Miller, Lynette Hardin, Sandra Naron, Patricia Naron, Martha Baird and Joyce Gann. Manager Penny Cox on left, Brenda Robertson on right.

Right: HHS girl's basketball team of 1961 was the first Houston team to win the Little Ten Conference, Sub District and District Tournaments and to advance to the North Half and State level. Sally Neal was the first person from Houston to be named an All-Star Guard. L-R: Molly Neal, Rebecca Smith, Sally Neal, Coach Joe Brigance (had just been diagnosed with Hodgkin's Disease), Jo Carolyn Harrington, Martha Moore and Kitty Simpson.

Jean Anne Hawkins "The Champ." Her record of successful free throws in a game still stands.

Houston Pee-wee Football Team. Front L-R: Jack Wilson, Eddie Dalton, Ralph Thomas, Glen A. Simpson, ?. Second row L-R: Robert Weaver, Rex Collins, Johnnie Smith, Eddie Dale Stafford, Bobby Dean Alford, Ed Gore, Kenneth Nichols and Dan Smith. Back row: Donald Gene Gann, Paul E. Kimble, Walter Blansett, Billy Ray Cole, Bill Winters, Allen Holliday, John Brand, and Donald Byrd ?

Ronald Barry Young of Houlka (1948-1985) was the first Chickasaw County All-State MHSAA boy's basket-ball player, 1966. Pictured here with Coach James (Shorty) Turner.

After a 40-27 win over Clay High in the finals of the Bi-county tournament, members of the 1962-63 Woodland Basketball team are treated to a steak dinner at the Post Office Cafe, compliments of Mr. Pete Wiggs. Back row L-R: Brenda Hampton, Charlotte Whitt, Mackey Woodruff, Erin Jennings, Betty Norris, Barbara Eaton, Pete Wiggs, Rebecca Box, Coach Billy Caples, standing, Lavon Caples, Betty Eaton, Phyllis Lancaster, Virginia Hampton and Dorothy Whitt.

Jack Gregory, Jr. of Okolona played ball at Delta State, University of Chattanooga and was drafted by the Cleveland Browns in their 1967 season. He later played for the New York Giants. He is a member of the Univ. of Chattanooga Athletic Hall of Fame and the Mississippi Athletic Hall of Fame.

John Gregory, son of Jack Sr. and Earline Gregory played ball for the Univ. of Mississippi where he played offensive tackle from 1970-72. He was selected to the SEC All Academic Team.

Kathy Young Davis, (presently Superintendent of Education at Houlka, MS) No. 2, was on the 1969 Houlka Wildcat team which placed third in the state. Joyce Box is on right, small boy is Michael Young (1957-1981); boy behind Kathy is Johnny Young.

Rogers Criddle, Chickasaw Academy Jr. High basketball, 1977-78. He received 1981 Coaches Award and N Central "A" All Tourney Award.

Gary Young Griffin was the first Houston High School golfer to be State MHSAA Medalist in 1981.

Ashley Stevens, Okolona Chieftain, is flanked by his parents, Harold and Jeanette Stevens at the 1985 All Star Game in Jackson, MS.

Larry Mosley, Chickasaw County professional bull rider, successfully riding a bull that had been attempted by others 66 times. He went to National Finals 10 consecutive years, finished second place each year. He rode the "Bull of the Year" five times.

Winners of an early 1980s Houston Country Club golf tournament. L-R: Tommy and Kay Y. Griffin, Bettye C. and David Thomas, Paul and Joan Uhiren, Dr. Thomas Powell and Don McCullough.

HHS Basketball State Champs, 1985.

Left: Jason Rish (Jake) Holladay at the 1996 National High School Finals Rodeo in Pueblo, CO.

Right: Lan Gooch of Houston qualified for PGA Tour in 1998.

The HHS Topper baseball team, District Champs in 2000.

Boyce Edward Clardy III "Trey," grandson of Rose and Kenneth Nichols, won first place in Mississippi High School Rodeo Bare Back Bronc Riding, 2002.

OUR PEOPLE WHO SERVED

William Rufus Kendall, (1838-1924), enlisted in MS 13th Infantry, 1861. Wounded at first Fredericksburg then again at Gettysburg where he was left behind when Lee's army withdrew. Exchanged and discharged in November 1863, he returned to Chickasaw County and married Mary Margaret Eskridge in April 1864, at Bethel Baptist Church.

Charles Wesley Kendall (1845-1910) enlisted in MS 6th Cav. in Houston in 1863. Captured and later exchanged into MS 13th Infantry where he served until surrender of Lee's Army of Northern Virginia in April 1865. Wounded at The Wilderness and at High Bridge, Virginia.

Absolom Skelton (1827-1905) son of Dozier and Cintha Skelton, Civil War veteran.

Matthew Benjamin Neal in his CSA uniform. He enlisted in 1861, killed near West Point, MS, in 1865.

Edmond C. Streeter 1844-1927 A veteran of the Mississippi 42nd Infantry, Co. G, CSA, shot in the ankle resulting in one leg being shorter than the other

Jeremiah King

Civil War veterans, seated L-R: John Carter, Gregory Blissard, Josiah Clark and Jonothan O. Clark. Standing L-R: Lude Lowery, Jim White and John Morgan.

Richard Puckett Gullett, Civil War veteran, was later a store owner at Center Grove (Now Mantee). Father of Samuel F. Gullett.

Ruel Vance

Lee Horn, Sgt. Quartermaster Corps, World War I

Pat Clark, about 1916 in WW I uniform.

Columbus Doss Lowry, US Navy, 1918

A.D. and A. J. Harrington, Jr., brothers in World War I.

John Wilkinson Jemison, Sr., USMC, between the wheels somewhere in France, WW I.

Charles William "Charlie" Anderson, Sr., U.S. Cavalry, World War I.

Tommy Lewis Pumphrey, WW I

Lynn Alford, World War I

Samuel Mack Ford, (1892-1972) World War I, Quartermaster Co.

Private Samuel Guy Smith, World War I

Tom McIntosh

Odell Porter, World War I

Columbus Doss Lowry, somewhere in Europe in 1918. He was a cook on a mine ship and was the son of Alfred Rushing Lowry.

Walton Blissard and Pat Clark just prior to leaving to fight in WW I

Amer Neal, (?), B. C. Hill and Cleve Doss at an American Legion Convention, about 1937-38.

WW II soldier Kenneth "Buck" Davis in front of a circa 1940 Chevrolet.

Bill and Naomi Nichols with their children, Lavelle and Bonnie Sue in St. Augustine, FL, 1940s.

James Dudley Brown

Bedford Forrest Dendy. 1915-1951; U.S. Navy, World War II

It's 1942 and Woodrow Cook of the Thorn Community stands by a John Deere tractor from the 1920s.

William David Sykes, Chickasaw County's first WW II casualty, was the son of Mr. and Mrs. A.J. Sykes. His obit in the Commercial Appeal of June 7, 1942, states that he was "killed at sea, somewhere in the war zone." The Houston VFW is named in his memory.

Henry Higginbotham, 1942

Ted Brown

Atwell Wooldridge, US Navy during WW II.

Barney O. Lowrey, 19 years old, US Navy

Edward Auston "Son" Martin, 1942

Cecil and Avery Langley, sons of Will and Sally Langley, both WW II veterans.

David Alford, US Army

Henry Higginbotham on left front, Lemual Moore standing on left.

Ervin Wall, December 1942

Charles Brown

Leon Curtis Neal, Jr., MSGT, US Marines in 1943, holding twin sisters Molly and Sally Neal.

William Edward Jemison, II; M/Sgt. Retired, United States Air Force, veteran of WW II, Korea and Vietnam era.

Edward Lee Taylor, March 1943 at Leesville, Louisiana.

William B. (Billy) Atkinson, 1943

Brothers Milford and James Welch get together in Ireland for a picture during WW II.

Charlie Guinn Griffin, member of 61st Infantry.

"Just Ether Duke and his Uke"

Chester Weldon Harrington (1916-1981), veteran of WW II, served with the US Navy Seabees in the Pacific. He was married to Corrinne Weaver and was the father of Faye, Jo and Gayle Harrington.

Walker Davis, World War II

On Sunday morning, Aug. 10, 1943, William Thomas Eaton (1913-1988), a corporal with the 312th Bombardment Group of the US Army is pictured at the first contact with the natives of Port Moresby, New Guinea. Eaton joined 9-7-42, discharged 10-22-45.

Elkin Woodruff, US Navy, 1943; served in the Pacific Theater.

Paul Rainey Chenault, U S Army, returned home from WW II in April 1944, and for the first time saw his son Danny Paul, born November 1942 to Mary Catherine Wilson Chenault (Walls, Griffin). Rainey's father served in World War I, Danny would later serve in Vietnam.

Reed Franks

Ralph Dexter at the Duxford Air Force Base in England, 1944.

Walker Lancaster

Lelon Melton outside barracks during WW II.

Curtis Spencer

Maurice Welch

Cpl. Walter A. Nabors of Houston

John Clifton Kendall, son of Robert Clifton and Lillie Mae Hawkins Kendall, with his sweetheart Elaine Dulaney at the old water fountain in front of the Pyland School. He was killed at sea, August 1944.

Harold Martin, 1944 in France. Harold was in Co. "C," 876th Airborne Engineering Aviation Battalion. He served 28 months in the European Theatre.

Grady W. Barnett, veteran of World War II was a Prisoner of War for 2 years and 2 months.

Durell C. Gann, a soldier in Troop A, 42nd Squadron, 2nd Mechanized Cavalry, landed in England June 29, 1944.

SP5 Jack Wilson, U.S. Army, propped on an appropriate sign.

Hubert Baird, 1945

Elias (Son) Weaver, Jr., husband of Jonnie McGowan; father of Robert, Mackie, Margie, Barbara Sue and Karen Weaver.

Nora Maxine Weaver, 1945. She was a WAC in World War II and was the daughter of Elias and Mace Canipe Weaver.

Hollis Randolph Pilgreen (1915-1976) served as a mechanic in the Army Ordinance Dept. from 1942-1945 in Europe. Born in Okolona, he was the ninth child of Frank James and Maida Viola Pilgreen.

Robert H. Thompson, WW II

Oliver James Volk, World War II

Willie Edd Murray

Charles William Anderson, Jr., at age 19, entering U.S. Navy in 1945.

Floyd Eaton and Sarah Clements in 1946.

Grady Williams, U.S. Army, 1947

Valine Dendy Pulaski, a member of the U.S. Army (Women's) in World War II.

Chickasaw County folks get together in Japan, ca 1948 or 1949. Back L-R: William Dreifus Kendall, Billy Joe Cook, T.J. Hulsey. Front L-R: ?, Raymond Turman and Robert Hawkins Kendall.

Daniel F. (D. F.) Wilson, US Army Air Corps, World War II

William H. "Bill" Patch, WWII; POW in Germany for 8 months.

Ira H. Clark

Leroy Clark

L-R: Henry Doss, Herbert Criddle, A.J. Huffman and Robert P. Huffman.

Rex Harrington

Maynard Clark

Woodrow Cook, 1st Armored Div., World War II

PFC Roscoe S. Smith, World War II, European Theater

T/Sgt. Mary Mildred Jemison, USMC. Houlka class of 1942; veteran of WW II, and Korea. Daughter of John Wilkinson Jemison Sr. and grandaughter of Wm. Edward Jemison (Luck).

Charles Wilson, home on leave, visits with Adie Sykes at Pyland, MS.

Two brothers get together in Japan to have a picture made for their mama - Thomas Hollie Kendall (left) and Robert Hawkins Kendall.

Donald Elkin Murray

Right: Durell C. Gann served the US Army as a driver of a mortar jeep. Pictured here after having been on the Rhine for 21 days, prior to the Battle of the Bulge in France.

William Hurd (Billy) Sanderson, Son of James K. Vardaman (Boozie) Sanderson and Annie Mae Guinn Sanderson.

T.J. Hulsey–picture was made in Japan shortly before he was shipped out to Korea. He was killed in action there.

Co. B, 114th Combat Eng Bn as it looked January 1950. From the top and L-R: R.H. Baine, C.C. Davis, J.T. Bray, S.B. Rieves, R.E. Walters. First row: D.H. Baine, R.P. Davis, M.E. Bounds, R.M. Brown, J.C. Callahan, T.H. Craig, G. Crocker, J.L. Doss, T. Doss, W.L. Estell. Second row: E.J. Hall, A.L. Hardin, T.A. Hardin, D.J. Huffman, R.L. Kendall, T.H. Kendall, W.D. Kendall, W. McCoy, J.W. Nelson, C.A. Spencer. Third row: R.C. Wilson, W.C. Blue, T.W. Clements, M.M. Cole, H.F. Coleman, C. ?Pumphrey, J.E. Rhodes, C.L. Harrington, O.K. Hightower, H.W. Kimble, J.E.Naron, Wm. Peel, E. Springer, J.A. Sykes, C.F. Thweatt, J.E. Warnick, G.E. Springer, R.S. Allen, D.E. Coleman, G.S. Avent, J.D. Wiggs. Fourth row: J.W. Collums, R.L. Criddle, J.D. Doss, ? Dulaney, T.R. Hinton, J.R. Mooneyham, P.R. Smith, G.A. Neal, W.R. Neal and L. Houser.

Russell Kendall (R) receives a commendation while serving with the Military Assistance Advisory Group in Formosa, 1952 or 1953.

Cpl. James M. (Jimmy) Smith, Kaiserslautern, Germany, 1954.

Travis Odell Williams, Korea, 1954

Okolona National Guard at Camp Shelby. Front L-R: John Callahan, L.R. Ross, Henry Ballard, Joe Bowen, Jr. Westmoreland, Glenn Pickens, Kenneth Coleman, Skeet Ellis, Melvin Maharrey, Tommy Woods, Buck Carlisle. Back L-R: Capt. Dorsey, Howard Lee O'Barr, Vaughn Hood, ? Whitt, Ronnie Williams, Gene Dallas, Edward Armstrong, Mabry Allison, Hunter Neubert, Harold Stevens, Billy Maharrey, Sid Whitlock, Thomas Clark, Guy Ellis Weeks, Fred Sullivan, Cecil Loyd, Hal Patterson, James Edward Edens, Rhynhart Neubert and Ray Boone. Picture made about 1954 or 1955.

Brothers Jesse Earnest of the U.S. Army and Tony Earnest of the U.S. Navy, 1958.

Captain J.T. Bray, Co. D, 223rd Engineer Bn. Camp Shelby Summer Camp in the early 1960s.

Russell L. Kendall of the U.S. Army and his son, Robert O. Kendall of the U.S. Navy visit at Pyland, Mississippi.

Jackie Houser and James Davis Doss at Ft. Polk, LA, 1961.

Grady Williams, a veteran from earlier times, says good-by to his son, Micheal, as he leaves for Vietnam.

Donald Murray in Vietnam in the 1960s.

Korea, early 1960s. Spec 5 Jack D. Wilson and special friend "Skosh" at military base. Skosh was provided food, clothing and expenses for school by Jack and other soldiers. Burial expenses were also provided when Skosh drowned in the Han River.

Air Force Captain Samuel T. Gore, left, is welcomed as flight leader of the first group of new F-5 fighter jets delivered to the US Air Force for testing at Eglin AFB, FL. In addition to his testing of the F-5, Sam flew 167 combat missions in Vietnam and was awarded the Air Force medal with six Oak Leaf Clusters and the Distinghished Flying Cross.

Corporal Gene Smith in Korea, about 1969-70.

James Robert Clark, son of James Edward and Glenda Clark.

SSG Kenneth M. Nichols, Co D -223 Engr. Bn. Houston, MS.

Members of Co. A, 223rd ENBN in Honduras, 1991. Front L-R: Larry Nichols, Richard Byars, Hervey Heard ?, Lawrence Knox, James Webb, Joe Lancaster. Back L-R: Bobby Roberts, Russell Verell, Dewey Cox, William Criddle, Leonard (Sonny) Gann and Tommy Robertson.

HISTORIC BUILDINGS

The A.K. Craig home, north of Houston, probably the oldest house still standing in Chickasaw County. Built around 1837.

R.W. Chandler home, built in 1850s, Prairie Street, Okolona.

J.L Rubel home, build in 1849 or 1850, Prairie Street, Okolona.

The home of James Pounds and Kate Sanderson Tabb, built in 1909. Destroyed by fire in 1928, the home greatly resembled his father's home built across the street and the present home of Bob and Ruth Kendall.

The corner of Main and Silver Street in Okolona, circa 1905. The row of buildings was built by "Capt." Frank Burkitt, owner and publisher of The Okolona Messenger. *The sign on top reads "Burkitt's Messenger." Other businesses in this building included a jewelry store and Burkitt's printing shop as well as the U.S. Post Office.*

The Judge Wm. S. Bates home is Houston's only surviving antebellum home. Built between 1830-1840, it was purchased by Judge Bates in 1861. His daughter, Scottie Bates Tabb, is seated on the steps.

The Henry Nichols house, Anchor Community, built about 1915.

The O. E. Baird home on Starkville Road, completed in April 1921.

The old Rueben Davis home in Houston, MS.

The Cecil Linn home, 443 South Jackson, Houston; built 1944-45 and is now the Houston Funeral Home.

Home of Alonzo T. and Ola House.

The John Paden home in Houlka, MS.

Houston Hotel, once located at the SE corner of the intersections of Highways 8 and 15. Built in 1905, it was taken down in 1955 after being purchased by an oil company.

The B.C. Hill home on North Jackson Street; present site of McDonalds.

Edens/Humphrey house, Okolona, MS. Built in the late 1800s by James Edward Edens, Sr. and wife Hattie Frazee Edens. Mr. Edens utilized the acres around his house in his cattle business. Easy access to rail service allowed him to ship to Memphis and New Orleans. Bro. and Mrs. J.E. Rogers purchased the house in 1953. In 1991 their granddaughter Brenda Humphrey and husband Dana purchased the house and restored it. In the house is hand carved front door, china cabinet, mantles. The original parquet floor imported from England is in the entry hall.

The house that D.D. Tabb (1846-1914) built in 1904 on Pontotoc Street. An example of early 1900 architecture, it is the present house of Bob and Ruth Kendall. According to his grandson, Jim Hugh Tabb, D.D. personally chose every tree used in construction.

The home of the Rev. Thomas Jefferson Lowry, located about 2 1/2 miles south of Houston.

The "Brogan Home" on what was originally the Brownlee Plantation in Chickasaw County.

Houston High School, Houston, MS, 1927-1973.

Home of A.F. (Buck) Huffman and Vida O'Barr Huffman, built before 1920.

Old Chickasaw County Jail in Okolona, picture made in the 1960s.

These buildings on the south side of the courtsquare in Houston have housed a telephone office, the Chester Davis Grocery, Snooty Owl Dress Shop, dentist office of Dr. Stublefield, Tabb Drug Store, and Tressie Berry's beauty shop. Picture made 1997.

On the left is the home of Walter E. Scott, Sr. (1905) and Walter E. Scott, Jr. (1937) as they looked on North Jackson Street, Houston.

Houston's old jail as it looked in 1970; new jail in the background.

Houston's Masonic Lodge, built circa 1929 and taken down in 1997; located at the present site of the First Methodist Church's Family Life Center, corner of Jackson and Hamilton Street.

BUSINESSES

Hickman Livery Stable, Houston, MS, owned by William P. Hickman and located about the present site of police station. Picture made circa 1900.

King's Grocery and Merchantile in Egypt, MS.

Inside view of J.B. Hasting - General Merchandise, about 1915. J.B. is behind the counter of the business, located at the GM & O Railroad depot.

Old Oil Mill, located across tracks west of G M & N Railroad Station in Houston, former site of City Maint. Shop. James P. Tabb is second from left; D.D. Tabb fourth. W.A. Tabb on right end. Boy is either Featherston or Jim Hugh Tabb.

V.A. Page in front of his Houston Produce Co., 1918; located at the present site of the U.S. Post Office in Houston.

John Harris Pearson at his store in Houston in the 1920s.

James Edward Edens, Sr. (1861-1937) of Okolona, was succeeded in the cattle business by his son, J.E. Jr., followed by grandson James Edward III, who still operates the business with the assistance of two sons, J.E. IV (Ed) and Lee Alderson Edens.

In the 1920s, J.B. Hasting had moved his business one block east of the courtsquare, where Aaron's Cleaners is now located. Far left is William Ira Seay, second from right is J.B. Hastings; others unidentified.

O.E. Baird and Brothers Machinists and Blacksmith Shop, 1922. L-R: Earl E. Baird, Osma E. Baird, John Parker and Will Parker.

E.L. Borden in front of his blacksmith shop in Okolona, MS; date unknown.

Crumps Dry Cleaners, date unknown.

Marion Luther Lancaster started his business in 1929 as a road salesman selling Watkins and Raleigh products.

Hill Hardware, Houston, MS. L-R Frank Byars, J.W. Hill, George Cox, ?, John W. Hill and Edgar Hightower.

Lee Horn came to Houston in 1919, worked with Sellar Smith and V.A. Page at Houston Produce. He and Page bought the business and moved to the north side of the square in early 1920s. In 1923, he bought out Page and changed the name to Horn's Grocery and moved to the west side of the square in the original Star Motor Co. building.

William Bates Tabb in his drugstore, date unknown.

D.L. Berry in the "Tea Room" as it used to be on East Madison Street.

Photo of a painting of the gas station and grocery store in Buena Vista owned by Jim and Cornelia Trenor. One of the earliest of its kind in the 1920s.

Wilson and Co. Cheese Plant, Okolona, MS, 1935.

Ford Agency, circa 1938, in Houston (present site of Clark Appliance). L-R: Cecil Linn, owner; wife, Louise C. Linn with son Jack; Doris Paden, secretary; Richard Paden, salesman; Kimble Blissard, Walter White, Hugh McBride, ?, Brezzie Harris, mechanic; little boy on right is Ray Green.

Ford Agency in Houston in the late 1930s. Present site of Clark Appliance.

Scott's Cash Grocery delivery man, "Jim," in his wagon; north side of the square in Houston, 1939.

Interior of John H. Pearson's store in Houston. Located where Telecap is at present.

Charlie Anderson's Mule Barn, about 1940. L-R: Charles "Buck" Carlisle under light pole, Charles Anderson, Jr., Charles Anderson, Sr., Jim Anderson and Clarke Carlisle. Horse is "Legion." Present site of Bill's Dollar Store.

An exterior view of the Flight 21 Restaurant in Houston, MS.

Flaherty's Store, Highway 15 North, about 1940.

The old Chevrolet dealership in Houston, corner of Jefferson and Madison Streets. L-R: ? Andrews, Frank Andrews, Charles Davis, Jim Reid, Jack Chenault and Leroy Andrews.

Gus Pearson in front of his store that served the needs of many customers in Houston. Located near the Rice-Stix factory, it was a convenient stop for groceries and other items.

Kraft Cheese Company in Houston.

Inside "Tabb Drugstore." L-R: unknown clerk, Mrs. Virginia M. Tabb, Wm. Bates Tabb and "Os" Walker. The headline of "Drug Topics" at end of counter reads "Save tin scrap to beat the Jap."

Robert Pearson's country store at McCondy, MS, in the late 1940s.

Dudley Russell "Tump" Brown, in his "Brown's Grocery" on Hwy. 15 N of Houston.

Uras and Dean Denton's country store, located at the corner of Hwy. 32 and County Road No. 1 in Chickasaw County; built in 1935 and closed in 1990.

Clark's Rolling Store with its barrell of kerosene on the back.

Flenoy Clark's Rolling Store by "The Justice Co. Wholesale Groceries" in Houston.

Horn's Grocery on the west side of the square in Houston.

Sale Day at the Chickasaw Commission Co. in Houston–Jasper Rish, auctioneer; ticket writer is Truman Pierce from Tupelo; Frank Weaver sitting on the ledge.

"Son" Weaver, in the ring at his Chickasaw Commission Co. shortly after moving to the new location in Houston. W.O. Johnson from Mantee is bottom row left behind Son; Hester Clark's head and hat is just behind Son; Verdie Griffin is to right of alley in hat and overalls.

Houston Redi-Mix Concrete Plant, off Hwy. 15 North in Houston.

The "Ice Plant" in Houston.

In 1946, E.F. Dyer moved his mill from Van Vleet to this location in Pyland, MS. In front is his daughter, Mable Dyer Hollowell, his wife Oral Floy Edwards Dyer, holding on to Mable's daughter Betty H. Davis; and on the right is Sallie Stoner.

Serving the needs of the Pyland Community, E.F. Dyer's Grocery was in business for many years. The benches in front were a place for visiting and Pan Am gasoline available for the autos.

Houston Cotton Gin, Hwy. 8 West; east of the railroad overpass, demolished in 1973.

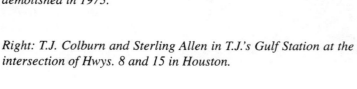

Right: T.J. Colburn and Sterling Allen in T.J.'s Gulf Station at the intersection of Hwys. 8 and 15 in Houston.

C.C. (Cap) Mixon's store, in the Anchor Community, opened for business in 1946. Groceries, feed, seed, fertilizer, dry goods, toys and gas were sold. It was also a voting precint and a place to visit with neighbors.

L-R: William (Shorty) Kilgore, Leland Norman, Sr. and Connie Lee Hill in front of the old B.C. Hill Funeral Home.

Houston's "Ben Franklin Store" at it's grand opening in 1950. In the foreground is Betty Jane Harrington, back of her is Esta Clark, ?, ?, and Albert Horn.

The C.C. "Cap" Mixon family inside their store, C.C. Mixon Gen. Mdse. on Hwy. 15, south of Houston in the Anchor Community, early 1950s. L-R: C.C. "Cap" Mixon, Virgie Dobbs Mixon, Bobby Mixon and Joan Mixon Lancaster.

J.L. (Jim Boy) Kendall's West End Grocery about 1950 or earlier. Helper is Preacher Putman.

James "Soup" Kyle with daughter, Margaret Ann Kyle Peel, in front of "Soup's Place."

Left: Judy and Dianne Kyle in front of Dave Kyle's "Snow Cone" in early 1950s.

Right: Smith Stave Company, located on old Highway 8 near its intersection with Pearl Street.

Unidentified customer sits at the counter of "Flight 21" restaurant in Houston, about 1952. Waiting to serve, l-r, is Joyce Sumner, Barbara Kendall (Harrington), Lucille and Roy Betts.

General Electric "Train Load Sale" at Chandler Furniture in Okolona, 1954. Chandler's Furniture and Undertaking was begun by R.W. Chandler, father of Cliff and grandfather of Walter. L-R: Jim Darden, Walter Chandler and his father, Cliff Chandler.

Left: Patch Piano Co. on Hwy. 15 South in Houston.

Right: Herman Smith, born in Vardaman, MS, started his dental practice in Houston in 1955. He practiced for 45 years. Mrs. Elaine Trenor was secretary and office manager for 35 years.

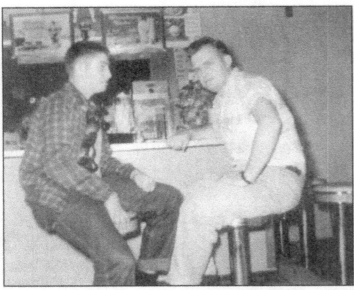

Oliver (L) and Jim Dick Nelson at Houston Drug Store around 1955; now Pearson's Drug Store.

Dendy's Department Store, west side of the square in Houston, operated by T.J. and Nellie Rose Dendy from 1955-1975.

Doy Cecil Corley in the store he and his wife, Grace Gilliam Corley, owned on Hwy. 32 West, 3 miles from Okolona. Picture made in the 1960s.

June 1963 at Wimberly Motors in Houston. L-R: Cameron Pumphrey, salesman; Ted Brown, salesman and G.D. Wimberly, president.

Management of Burris Industries of Prairie, MS, in 1965. Seated: Byron Wilson, Plant Manager. Standing L-R: Buck Kennedy, Plant Superintendent; Murry Whitt, Frame Supervisor; Brewer Henley, Purchasing; Gary Young, Purchasing Manager and Joe Criddle, Corporate Engineer. All management, except Henley, were from Chickasaw County.

At the Chickasaw Handle Company, established in 1946 by James McCullough, Elbert Hensley, Thurman Lowe and Frederick Swan, logs begin the process of becoming handles and other wood turnings.

The finished product-handles and other wood turnings ready to be shipped from the Chickasaw Handle Company to all parts of the country and many locations worldwide. The company was sold and moved in 1990.

Oris W. Lancaster in front of his fruit and vegetable market that he began in 1950.

Frances and David Wilburn Allen at their store in Buena Vista, MS, about 1970.

Houston Ceramic Tile, Christmas Party, December 9, 1972. Front, L-R: Gretchen Bradberry, Bobbie Nell Pumphrey, Pauline Pounds, Effie M. Brand, Martha Nell Martin, Ludean Vaughn and Coriene Moore. Back, L-R: William Eaton, Mary Wilson, Harold Frasier, Myra Hancock, Jimmie Collums, Annette Logan, Wanda Walters, Floyd Reese, Robert Melton, Cecil Peppers and William (Bill) Yeager.

CARSON'S DEPARTMENT STORE

In May of 1975, Pam Miskelly Carson and Charles Marion Carson III became the proud owners of Carson's Department Store at 111 N. Jackson Street, Houston, Mississippi.

The Carsons both came from a retail background. Chuck's grandfather operated a store in Yazoo County for many years. Pam's parents owned and operated Howard's Department Store in Okolona, Mississippi, for 40 years.

Many of their store fixtures were obtained from both of these establishments.

Although the Carsons have been in business for 27 years, the business dates back to 1933, when Mr. Turner Ray established Ray's Cash Store. He operated this business until 1956 when he sold the business to Mr. T.J. Dendy. Mr. Dendy and his family operated Dendy's Department Store until 1975 when he sold the store to the Carsons.

In 1995 the Carsons expanded their business and moved next door to the old Western Auto and Ben Franklin buildings at the current 115 N. Jackson Street location.

A desire to provide quality clothing and shoes at affordable prices for the entire family has been their goal.

Chuck and Pam Carson

CHICKASAW EQUIPMENT COMPANY

Chickasaw Equipment Company was founded in the late 1940s as a Ford Tractor dealership. F.T. "Red" and Mary Ann Alford bought the business in 1964 from W.J. Linn. At that time the business was located in the building that is now Frank Smith's Body Shop. The tractors and equipment were located on the east side of Highway 15 where Pizza Hut and Pak-a-Pok are now located. In 1974, a new building was built on the present site about two miles north of town on County Road 31. Red and Mary Ann operated the business until October 1990 when they sold it to Frank and Donna Alford.

The dealership has seen many changes over the last sixty years. In the beginning, the customer base was made up primarily of full-time farmers. During the 1980s the customer base began to change to more part-time farmers, especially cattle farmers. These were people with off-farm income that were involved with cattle, timber or just maintaining their land for other uses such as hunting. In 1986 Chickasaw Equipment Company became the first Polaris ATV dealer in the state of Mississippi. This helped the dealership increase its customer base and provided sales and service work during the winter months.

The philosophy at Chickasaw Equipment Company has always been to "service what we sell" and to "treat people like we want to be treated." This has served the dealership well as it has seen continued growth. God has truly blessed both generations of the Alford family with loyal customers and faithful employees.

Mark Alford, son of F.T. and Mary ann Alford on tractor.

CHICKASAW MILLING COMPANY

Chickasaw Farm Services, located at 630 West Church Street, Houston, Mississippi, serves as both retail outlet, as well as a garden and plant center.

In 1952, Jack Barett built a one room feed mill which became Chickasaw Milling Company, located at 627 West Church Street, Houston, Mississippi. This mill had a hammermill, which ground ear corn, corn stalks, peanut vines, hay and milo. He also had a mixer with which he custom made feed.

In 1954 he sold the business to Bill Baird and Allen Ware.

In 1955 Allen and Clytee and children, Frank, James, Barbara and Elizabeth bought out Mr. Baird. The purpose for buying the mill was to feed out 50,000 layers and 50,000 broilers. They also had an egg grading station in back of the store (now Beauty Pointe Salon). They ran the store which was Ware Bro.'s Feed and Seed. (now 389 Gro.) Floyd and Allen Ware were partners in this for two years, then Allen bought out Floyd's part and Floyd went to work at the milling company where he and Frank Smith Sr. were managers until 1958.

In 1956 an addition of three rooms was constructed.

In 1959 Jerry Ware, son of Floyd Ware, became the manager until 1963.

In 1964 Gus Hughes, son of L.B. Hughes became the manager. He and his father both worked there.

In 1965, Allen and Clytee came to the mill to run it themselves. Six months later, Frank Ware, their son, came to help his father.

In 1973 Frank and Jim Gordon became partners and bought out the mill. In 1974 Allen Ware died of cancer.

Jim and Frank were partners for eight years, during this time we grew more into the fertilizer, chemical and salt busi-

ness. We also made an addition across the street of a new office and large warehouse.

In 1980, Frank, Carolyn, Dana, Richard and Angela Ware bought out Jim Gordon's stock.

In 1983 an addition of a fertilizers blender to blend custom fertilizers.

In 1988 the old Houston Fertilizer was purchased from Delta Purchasing and Houston State Bank. The fertilizer and chemical operation was moved to that location on Franklin Avenue. Frank and Carolyn managed this location while Barry Dendy stayed behind to run the milling.

In 1990 Richard Ware became the manager of the mill.

In 1996 Frank and Carolyn sold the mill to Richard and Melissa, Ricky and Kaddy. The name was changed to Chickasaw Farm Services, Inc.

In 1996 Frank and Carolyn bought the Houlka Grain and Feed, Ronnie Vanlandingham and Will Terry ran the office and the name was changed to Chickasaw Farmers Grain, Inc.

In 1997 Frank and Carolyn sold the Chickasaw Fertilizer to Terra Inc. (Agro) In this same year they started a grain elevator in Houston and ran it.

In 1998 Frank and Richard began planning for a new mill.

In 2001 Frank and Richard combined businesses equally and became partners in Chickasaw Farm Services, Inc. and Ware Milling Co., Inc.

Employees are: Leon Ira Conner, Mahlon Gann, Bobby Holder, George Hughes, Anthony Hancock, Randy Hurst, Ray Johns, Barbara Kilgore, Sammy McGregor, Jim Nelson, Ronnie Smith, Des Smith, Jerry Vance, Carolyn Ware, Melissa Ware, Frank Ware, Richard Ware and James Wofford.

The new Ware Milling Company, Inc., a large manufacturing facility, located at 150 AFL Dr., Houston, Mississippi. (Construction began in 2001 and completed in 2002.)

CLASSIC FURNITURE MANUFACTURING
1231 CR 515 NORTH
HOUSTON, MISSISSIPPI 38851
662-456-5900

Classic Furniture Manufacturing Co. began operations in September of 1985 at 313 South Jackson Street in Houston. At the beginning there were only two full time employees and four part time. Only one style of upholstered living room furniture was made. Three-piece living room suits were built, loaded on a truck and sold, literally door to door at furniture stores. Often the truck would come back with one or two suits still on the truck. Soon customers began to call in orders.

In June of 1991, a new 10,000 square foot building was erected at our present location. This expansion allowed us to hire eight new full-time employees and expand to making many new styles of furniture.

In 1993, we expanded again by adding 10,000 square feet of warehouse space. In 1998, another 5000 square feet was added.

Presently Classic Furniture has 20 full-time employees. We now manufacture 16 different styles of living room furniture, along with occasional chairs, ottomans, and sleeper-sofas. We also now have furniture salesmen who sell our products to retail stores nationwide.

Since 1985 Classic Furniture has never had to layoff any employees. This is due to the high quality products our employees proudly build.

We would like to thank all our employees for their quality craftsmanship.

Frank, Dean and Patti Daniel

COLBERT AUTO WORLD
HWY. 8, WEST   HOUSTON, MISSISSIPPI
456-3756

From left: Andy Colbert, Neal Colbert and Mike Colbert.

Established in December of 1970 under the name of Colbert Petty Chevrolet-Olds, Inc., this family-owned business was begun by J.M. (Jay) Colbert, Ralph Petty and Cliff Colbert. Carl Lee Colbert also played a major role in this dealership.

In July of 1984, Mike Colbert, Neal Colbert and T.S. Colbert purchased the dealership from Colbert-Petty and changed the name to Colbert Auto World. In 1986, T.S. Colbert sold his stock in the company to Colbert Auto World and the company added a new partner, Andy Colbert.

Franchised lines for this dealership include Chevrolet, Oldsmobile, Buick, Pontiac and GMC Trucks.

Employees of many years who have played significant roles in the dealership are: Amy Files, Angela Capps, Chris Higginbotham, Wes Lowe, Chip Long, Rebecca Pruett, Harold Frazier, James Files, William Hamilton, Kitt Bryant, Dean Hill, Butch Mixon and Nina Watts.

In addition to the many retired drivers who have played a major role in molding this dealership, former employees include: Dewayne McQuary, Hubert Higginbotham, Becky Kilgore, Carl Lowry and Jimmy Rhodes.

DIXIE DINER
HOUSTON, MISSISSIPPI
1961-1982
CONTRIBUTED BY DAVID C. HORN

The Dixie Diner Cafe was opened by Ted and Ruby Horn in the spring of 1961 at the corner of Washington and Jefferson Streets on the NE corner of Pinson Square. The original location had once housed Manie Halls Store and is now part of BancorpSouth. The Cafe was open from 5:00 AM to 8:00 PM in its early days. Breakfast was a special treat since "The Houston Dairy Milk Route Boys" and other "early risers" usually showed up by 4:30 AM and were ready for coffee and some of Mr. Ted's fine food. A special treat was Mr. Ted's fried eggs. He had Hubert Baird make "rings" or perfect circles out of stainless steel. When a customer ordered "two over light, etc.," the rings were placed on the hot grill and the eggs broken into the rings, resulting in perfectly round fried eggs. Mr. Ted's breakfast plate was the most delicious breakfast serving I have ever seen. Of course a generous serving of "Grits with real butter" from the large steaming cauldron located next to the grill didn't hurt either. Many times "Yankee" visitors or travelers were persuaded to try "Grits" and the majority were pleased and astonished at the wonderful flavor, especially when they learned to stir their fried eggs into the grits, of this "Southern Food!" Mrs. Ruby would work her lunch hour (she worked for the Welfare Service) in order to help wait on customers. Lura Nichols, Donna Ray and Bonnie Houk worked as waitresses for many years and Mag Hamilton and Jean Jones worked as cooks and served up the "country cookin" the Dixie Diner was renowned for.

The Dixie Diner featured "Plate Lunches," a selection of several meats and generous servings of home cooked and often home raised vegetables with "homemade" dessert, for dine in or take out. In 1963, due to the crowds of customers, an additional dining room was added by cutting a doorway through the west wall (Dr. Thomas Gore's old office) and doubling the available dining space. There was also a dining room for black patrons located in the north side of The Diner and next to the kitchen. Mr. Ted worked many 16 hour days, six days per week and was open for lunch on Sunday for many years. He scaled back to just breakfast and lunch Monday through Saturday in 1968. Somehow even with this work schedule Mr. Ted managed to tend a large garden and became renowned, even after his "retirement" for the large and delicious tomatoes he raised and sold on Hwy. 15 North.

In 1965 Mr. Ted purchased a "Catering Truck" and in 1966 a second truck to transport hot and cold sandwiches, hot and cold beverages, snacks and hot "plate lunches" to factories and businesses in the Houston area. These trucks were always a welcome sight at Jackson/Shannon Mfg., M & P Mfg., Union Camp, Houston Hospital, Seminole Mfg., auto dealerships, feed mills, service stations and other businesses. Mr. Ted's son David and David's wife Pat, operated this portion of the "Ted Horn Food Service" until July 1968. Mr. Ted cut back to one truck and continued to operate the catering service until 1986. One would wonder just how many snacks, drinks and meals Mr. Ted served off those trucks in those 21 years of faithful service. It was said you could set you watch by the appointed time and arrival, winter, summer, rain or snow, of "Mr. Ted's Truck!"

In 1970 the Dixie Diner relocated to 100 West Madison Street so that Mr. Ted could scale back his business to a one man operation in The Diner. He was the cook, waitress, cashier, busboy, and dish washer! He retained one employee to prepare food for the catering truck in a separate building located in the "alley" behind The Diner.

The Dixie Diner, 100 West Madison Street

Mr. Ted operated The Dixie Diner until 1982 when he sold the business to another individual who opened a pizza parlor. Mr. Ted continued to operate the Ted Horn Food Service catering truck until 1986 when he retired so that he and Mrs. Ruby could "see the world!" The Dixie Diner building now houses the C & G Barber Shop.

It was in this location, in November 1971, that "THE MIRACLE OF 100 WEST MADISON STREET" occurred. This is the account of "THE $20.00 THAT WENT A LONG WAY" and gave rise to the generous philanthropic efforts of a man known only as "The Secret Santa!" The following is an account of this beautiful and wonderful story that began when Mr. Ted, through his own kindness and generosity, helped a young man, down on his luck and stranded, in Houston, without money for food or gasoline. This man went on to become a successful and wealthy industrialist who in appreciation for his "good fortune" became a "Godsend" to thousands of poor and needy people! Mr. Ted provided the "salvation" for this young man and thus "The Miracle" became a legend that proves yet again that God, our Lord and Savior, works in mysterious ways His wonders to perform! The following account is an excerpt from an article by Nancy Hellmich in *USA Today*, December 2001.

In late winter of 1971, Santa, then a young man, was working in the little town of Houston, Miss., as a door-to-door salesman. His company went out of business, and within a few days, Santa had no money for food, gas or the motel room he was renting.

He also had no family to turn to for help. So he went to a local church, where he was told that the person in charge was gone for the day and to check back tomorrow. "I was ashamed of being homeless. I was terribly embarrassed, and I didn't want anybody to know. I didn't go back."

For eight days, he slept in his car, he says. He didn't have a nickel to his name and hadn't eaten for almost two days when he went to a diner and ordered a big breakfast. He sipped his coffee until the crowd thinned out, then acted like he had lost his wallet.

I put on what I thought was an Academy Award performance. I fumbled around for my wallet. I got up and looked around the front door for it, and I looked around the stool I had been sitting on. I had this bewildered look on my face," Santa says.

Then the owner of the diner, who also was the waiter and cook, came over near

Ted and Ruby Horn

the stool where Santa had been siting and picked up a $20 bill on the floor. "Son, you must have dropped this," the diner owner said.

"It was like a fortune to me," Santa Says. "I said to myself, "Thank you Lord." And my next thought was that I'd better go ahead and get out of here before the person who really dropped it comes back in."

He paid for the breakfast, left a tip, pushed his car to a gas station and headed west.

On the way out of town, it dawned on him "that maybe nobody had dropped the money at all - maybe that fella just knew I was in trouble, and he helped me in a way that didn't embarrass me.

"I'd been praying for a few days before that, and right then I just made a little promise. I said, "Lord, if ever you put me in a position to help other people, I will do it."

Within a year he had packed all of his belongings into one suitcase and headed to Kansas City on a bus. He struggled for years to make a living. He got married and had children. "I borrowed money to start a business and sweated blood to pay it back," but it failed, he says. A second business, however, was successful.

It was 1979 when he made good on his promise to help those less fortunate. On a cold, snowy day around Christmas in Independence, Missouri, he stopped at a drive-in and ordered a hamburger and soft drink. He gave the carhop a $50 bill and said, "Keep the change."

You're kidding," she said.

"No Ma'am. Merry Christmas," he said.

She started sobbing and said, "Sir, you have no idea what this means to me."

It felt so wonderful that Santa went directly to the bank, got some more cash and started giving it away, he says.

For a few years he didn't tell a soul what he was doing, not even his wife and children. Now, his whole family is in on it, and he and his wife budget how much they can afford to give away. One year alone he handed out $85,000. Over the past 22 years, he figures, he has given away hundreds of thousands of dollars. He says there are no tax breaks for the way he distributes his money.

In 1999 he returned to Mississippi and found the owner of the diner who had given him $20. Santa said at the time that $20 seemed like $10,000 to him, so he gave the then elderly gentleman whose wife was ailing $10,000.

DIXIELAND MANUFACTURING COMPANY

DixieLand Manufacturing Company was established in April 1976 with three owners: Leon Martin, Charles Lancaster and Dean Holder. DixieLand makes living room furniture including sofas, love seats, chairs, recliners and sleepers. In 1992 Martin and Lancaster sold out, and Dean and Mary Holder became owners. Tim Finn, Plant Manager, and Randy Allen, Assistant Plant Manager, are the longest-term employees at DixieLand. Both started working at the plant at age 16, and worked after school until graduation. Following graduation both became full-time employees.

Tim Finn, Plant Manager
Randy Allen, Assistant Plant Manager

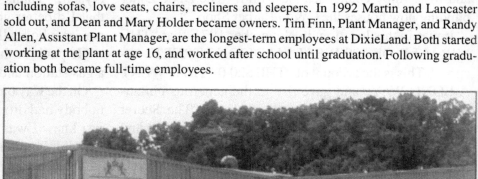

DixieLand today

Lisa Vanlandingham, office

Dorothy King, seamstress

J.C. Lyons, employed over 25 years

Sewing room

CHICKASAW COUNTY FARM BUREAU

Chickasaw County Farm Bureau began with the request for a Charter of incorporation signed by V.A. Page, M.H. Davis and J.E.. Atkinson all of Houston. The charter request was received and approved by Joseph W. Power, Secretary of State, on the fifteenth of February 1923.

The purpose of the incorporation as listed in the charter was "to promote and develop the best systems of production and marketing agriculture in all its forms and branches, and to plan and promote the social and economic welfare of those engaged in agriculture.

The first agents to work with Farm Bureau in Chickasaw County were A.E. Bland and Robert Carr. Jack Barret was named again in 1953. Shortly after that, Evans Dendy was appointed agent.

Mrs. Helen Brown was the first secretary to work for Farm Bureau in the Houston office. Then Sylvia Martin was hired and worked for about twenty years.

Don Cook was hired as an agent in 1976 and upon retirement of Evans Dendy, became the agency manager. Charlie Lee Griffin began serving as a Farm Bureau agent July 1, 1969. James "Butch" Griffin joined the Farm Bureau family in 1978. Tracy Whitt came aboard as an agent in 1983. In 1987 both Danny Buskirk and Dewitt Moore joined the staff as agents. Rick Huffman was hired as an agent in February of 1996.

Joyce Whitt worked as Farm Bureau County Secretary and Houston office secretary until retirement in 2001. Lela Norris was hired as secretary in the Houston Office in 1991 and upon Joyce Whitt's retirement, was appointed county secretary. Sara Palmer works in the Okolona office and Carla Spencer in Houston.

Chickasaw County Farm Bureau experienced several losses in 1988. On May 2, 1988, longtime agent Charlie Lee Griffin died of cancer. On May 24, 1988, an automobile accident claimed the life of former agency manager Evans Dendy and his wife, Elverna. Longtime employee, Sylvia Martin, died on November 14, 1988.

Agent James "Butch" Griffin who worked for 17 years, died on Sunday, September 10, 1995.

Over the years, there have been many who have worked with Farm Bureau in Chickasaw County and left us with good memories and

Chickasaw County Farm Bureau, Houston office

Chickasaw County Farm Bureau, Okolona office

good friendships. These include Ronja Shipley Lancaster, Glenda Spencer Chrestman, Regina Eaton Bullock, Gabriella Davis, Amy Anderson Jacobs and others. Agents who once worked with Chickasaw County Farm Bureau include Bill Henson and Paul Grubbs.

The board has always been very supportive of innovative programs that promote agriculture, home and farm safety, community pride and family values. Board members individually and as a group work hard to help bring about legislative changes that benefit the farmer and people all throughout the communities we serve. Their dedication to the people of our communities and to the agents who represent Farm Bureau and its insurance companies is greatly appreciated.

Chickasaw County Farm Bureau will continue to grow because of the hard work of its people and the advent of new products and services that promote agriculture,

economic development, and the strong family bond that has always been an integral part of Farm Bureau.

FARM BUREAU BOARD MEMBERS
(at the time of this writing)

Jan Dale Hill, President
Mike Langley, Vice-President
Jerry Criddle, Past President
Steve Pearson
Steve Pettit
Ronnie Vanlandingham
Jimbo Corley
Danny Clark
Bill Joe Rish
Charles D. Easley, Honorary Member
of the county Farm Bureau Board.

GANN'S CLOTHING

John L. Gann was born in Clay County, April 4, 1922, to John T. and Emma Brown Gann. After being drafted into the Army in December 1942, he received a medical discharge in November 1945.

John returned to his home in "Happy Hollow," near the confluence of the Houlka and Cane Creeks, just south of the Chickasaw-Clay county line. For the next five years he farmed with his father. John began working for Lawrence Harrington at a service station in Houston, located at the site of the present fire station.

In 1956 he and James Graydon Griffin purchased the old Studebaker Agency building from Sid Springer and opened an auto repair shop and service station. During the next 40 years John was involved in several businesses at this location. One was a trucking company. James G. Griffin and John Gann dissolved their business partnership and Griffin took over the trucking company while John continued the repair shop and service station.

In 1968 John and his wife Elizabeth Thompson Gann ventured into the sale of hunting, fishing and sporting goods along with the service station business. In 1972 they added clothing. To accommodate their growing business, they made additions in 1986, 1992 and 1993 with more than 8,000 square feet presently in use. The sporting business was sold in 1998 and since that time has consisted of clothing and shoes from infants to adult sizes.

Employees through the years include William O'Barr, Tom Pate, Howard "Wolf" Evans, Clem Shellie, James Shellie, Travis Harrington, Dick Griffin, Agnes Dendy, Jo Mixon, Tracey Kilgore, Samantha Fort, Dawn Marshall, Judy H. East, Mary Ann Peden, Theresa Hardin, Carol Uhiren, Lisa W. Kilgore, Cindy Lancaster and Nick Johnson.

After graduating from Mississippi State University, their daughter, Charlotte, became a partner in the business. Charlotte is married to Tim Birmingham and they have one child, Colton.

John Gann and grandson, Colton Birmingham.

222

GRIFFIN MOTORS INC.

925 N. JACKSON STREET   *HOUSTON, MS 38851*   *662-456-4281*

Purchased April 1, 1978, by Raymond and Charlotte Griffin, Griffin Motors has strived to serve the automotive needs of Chickasaw County for more than 20 years.

Raymond and Charlotte wish to honor their employees, past and present, with these photos.

From left: Joe Dobbs, Elvin Ferguson, Donald Dobbs, Frank Smith, Sam McWhirter, Gary Turner, Adolph Davis, John Flemings, Raymond Griffin, Wayne Buchanan, Charlotte Griffin, Bobby Gilbert, Brenda Eaton and Tommy Smith.

"Frosty" Criddle and Sam McWhirter

Bobby Gilbert and Gradis Whitt

Ronnie Cole and Joe Dobbs

B.M. Cole and Wayne Buchanan

Brenda Eaton

Bobby Sanderson

223

HOUSTON BUILDING SUPPLY

Houston Building Supply, Inc., a division of Nabors Hardware and Building Supply, Inc., opened in the Spring of 1985 at 125 Malcomb Street in Houston, Mississippi. It is a third generation family business which began in 1962 in Vardaman, Mississippi, with Harley V. Nabors as owner. In October 1969 Fred A. Nabors took over the business and made the move to Houston in 1985. Houston Building Supply opened with only six employees and over the past 17 years the business has grown to employ over 20 individuals. In 1998 Lee A. Nabors bought the business from his father and is the current owner.

Houston Building Supply is a full service building supply store which carries plumbing, electrical, paint, lawn and garden, lumber, plywood, windows and doors. A stand alone Do-It Best Rental Center opened in the winter of 1999. The rental center rents construction equipment such as backhoes, trenches, demolition equipment and painting equipment. It also has items for the do-it yourselfer such as carpet cleaners, floor finishing and lawn care.

From left: Fred Nabors, Fay Griffin Nabors, Henry Easley, Ronald Jordan, Lonnie Brand and Frank Thomas.

From left: Kenny Clemons, Frank Thomas, Fay Griffin Nabors, Fred Nabors, Penny Nabors Cochran and Lee Nabors.

Future

HOUSTON FUNERAL HOME

The Houston Funeral Home is one of Houston's oldest businesses. Now located at 443 South Jackson Street, its history is traced back to 1910.

In 1954 Mr. Leland Brown Norman, Sr. and his wife Louise Bullard Norman bought a funeral home from Mr. Avery Hill, who had bought it from his brother J.W. Hill. They names this business Norman Funeral Home.

The business was originally founded in 1929 by B.C. Hill, the then owner of B.C. Hill Hardware and Furniture Company. This was located in the building on the southwest corner of the town square. It was relocated in 1935 to the first floor of the historic Greentree Hotel which was on the north east corner of the square, now the location of Bill's Dollar Store. It was the area's first funeral home. The Normans also let the building be used by a group that later became the Parkway Baptist Church.

The move to the present location came in 1961 when the Normans purchased the Houston Funeral Home. This funeral business had been founded by John W. Hill, owner of the Houston Hardware and Furniture Company, in the days when undertaking establishments were often affiliated with other types of businesses. Mr. Hill founded this business in 1910.

The Normans retained the name Houston Funeral Home. In 1963 Mr. Norman passed away. Mrs. Norman continued in the business and was soon joined by her son, Leland Brown Norman, Jr. Mrs. Norman passed away in 1999.

The Houston Funeral Home is located in what had been the home of the late Cecil Lynn, built in 1948. This home is of particular historical significance because it was constructed of material taken from the girl's dormitory of the Buena Vista Agricultural College.

Houston Funeral Home is a member of the National Funeral Directors Association, The Mississippi Funeral Directors Association, and the International Order of the Golden Rule, an organization that recognizes only leading funeral homes. Leland B. Norman, Jr. has served as president of the Mississippi Funeral Directors Association, Chairman of the State Board of Funeral Service, and selected Funeral Director of the Year.

HOUSTON INSURANCE AND REAL ESTATE AGENCY
113 WEST WASHINGTON   HOUSTON, MS 38851
662-456-2511

Begun in the early 1920s by a Mr. Wilkerson, Houston Insurance Agency was located upstairs over Pearson's Drug Store. Since its beginnings, the agency has changed ownership several times. Some of the owners have been a Mr. White, Carter Patch, Harold and Edith Jones. Charles Chandler purchased the agency and is the present owner. From above the drug store, the agency has also been located under the Union Planters Bank building and was moved to its present location in the 1990s.

Many additional services were added in the 1990s, including real estate appraisals, real estate brokerage and investments as well as more lines of insurance.

Working to serve you at Houston Insurance are the following: Charles Chandler, Owner/Agent; Louis Chandler, Appraiser, Agent; Mickie Criddle, Agent, Sylvia Stone, Secretary; and Nell Chandler, Bookkeeper.

The agency is a member of the Independent Agents of Mississippi and America; the Professional Insurance Agents of Mississippi; National Association of Real Estate Appraisers and Mississippi Association of Realtors.

Allstate Insurance Company is Houston Insurance Agency's number one company and they offer a full line of insurance products.

Houston Insurance and Real Estate Agency has grown with the area and looks forward to growing and serving the Houston area for many more years.

HOUSTON MONUMENT COMPANY

Houston Monument Company was established by Leland B. Norman, Sr. and Louise Norman in 1961. After Mr. Norman's death in 1963, Mrs. Norman, Curtis Alford and V.O. Taylor ran the business until 1968. Lonnie Whitt went to work for Mrs. Norman in August of 1968. Mr. Whitt bought one-half interest in the business in 1971. In March of 1973, Mrs. Norman sold her share of the business to Mr. Whitt who has been sole owner since that time. Lonnie and V.O. Taylor ran the business until 1980 when Mr. Taylor became disabled.

When the business was established, it was located at 223 West Madison. In February 1990, the business was moved to new facilities at its present location, 616 West Madison Street (Highway 8 West).

Since 1980 the business has been run by Lonnie and Bonnie Whitt, Danny Sullivan, Eddie Neal, Bobby Catledge, Odie Bailey with James Willis and Alice Harmon working part-time.

This business has grown and prospered because of these people mentioned above and also because of many loyal customers.

MEMORIAL FUNERAL HOME
HOUSTON, MISSISSIPPI
THREE GENERATIONS IN FUNERAL HOME BUSINESS

Memorial Funeral Home in 1961.

Memorial Funeral Home was established in 1961 by William (Shorty) Kilgore and Mr. Howard White. After the death of Mr. Kilgore in 1968, Memorial Funeral Home passed to his wife, Frances.

At her retirement, the business passed to the Kilgore children: Robert (PeeWee) Kilgore and sisters Betty Kilgore Miller, Beth Kilgore Brown and Faye Kilgore Dendy.

In 1998, Memorial Funeral Home was purchased by Stacey and Melinda Dendy Parker. Now in its third generation of family service, Memorial Funeral Home strives to provide caring and professional service during a time of great need.

Shorty Kilgore

Frances Kilgore

PeeWee (1939-1999)

Betty, Faye, Beth, Frances and Robert (PeeWee)

Stacey and family

Memorial Funeral Home as it is today, 2002.

Memorial Funeral Home office, known as the old Metts house.

Our Founding Fathers

Ashton Toomer
First President

W.B. Funderburk
First General Manager

L.W. Harpole
First Vice President

George C. Mabry
Board Member

Lighting the way to the future

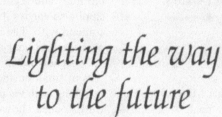

Joe T. Patterson
First Secretary
and Attorney

J.R. McCord
Board Member

Dr. J.M. (Jim) Hood
Board Member

Edward R. Creekmore
Board Member

Owned by the members it serves

Natchez Trace Electric Power Association was born December 19,1939. It came about because our founding fathers had not only a vision and a dream but also the motivation and knowledge to carry that dream to reality. Their goal was to eventually provide electricity to every family and business in the rural areas.

This task would not be easily accomplished. It would cost a lot of money to build lines and other facilities necessary to eventually supply power to parts of seven counties. Even if electricity were made available at a low cost, it would be difficult for some members to pay the $2 to $5 minimum monthly power bill because money was scarce. Some families were not interested because they were simply scared of electricity; therefore, a selling job was necessary to convince members to sign up.

The only reason the dream of an electric cooperative became a reality was because of two organizations formed in the 1930s. The Tennessee Valley Authority (TVA) was created in 1933 to provide cheap electric

power, flood control, and industrial development throughout the Tennessee River basin. The year 1935 brought the Rural Electrification Administration (REA) to provide electric power for rural America by offering low-interest loans made or guaranteed by the federal government. The REA made possible the rise and viability of electric cooperatives which would be owned by their consumers. As a note, Alcorn County Electric Power Association, located in Corinth, MS, was the first electric cooperative in the nation.

In 1939, life began to get better for people in this area as the opportunity to acquire electricity spread across the land. Today Natchez Trace serves electricity to more than 15,000 meters. While the association has changed over the years, it still operates with a cooperative spirit as it takes pride in providing low-cost and reliable electricity to its members. With branch offices in neighboring Calhoun and Webster Counties, the headquarters remains in the town of Houston in Chickasaw County.

NORTHEAST MS L.P. GAS CO., INC.

In 1945 Mr. D.B. Ellard and Mrs. Elizabeth Ellard pioneered the gas and appliance business in Houston that they named Northeast Mississippi L.P. Gas. Plans had been made to go into the business during the war. When the war ended these plans were put into motion. Tanks and equipment were hard to acquire because of the post World War II scarcity of materials.

Space was rented in the old Tabb Drug Store to display merchandise. Land was then bought on Highway 8 West where the present building is located. At one time army barracks were located on the land.

These barracks were used to house the business until material was available for a building in 1951.

As merchandise became available, Northeast Mississippi Butane Gas Co. began to stock the latest in butane heaters and burners and began installing tanks as they became available.

In 1972 the present modern building was built on the same location. The first truck used had a 1,068 gallon capacity compared to the present trucks which haul 2,600 gallons. Eddie Bounds, Elmo Bounds' father, was the first truck driver.

In 1972 Mr. and Mrs. Ellard's son, Craig, took over the business. Mr. and Mrs. Ellard continued to be involved until 1981 when Craig's wife, Melissa, joined him in the daily operations of the business.

James M. Neal, who was hired in 1952, retired in 1997 after 45 years of service. Mr. Neal was a valued employee and was highly respected in the industry.

In September of 1993, Bill Blissard began working with the company painting tanks and doing service work. He now is involved in the daily delivery of propane.

Terri Faulkner was hired in October 1995. She uses her accounting degree from Mississippi State University to perform the bookkeeping duties of the business.

In 1997 Catherine Landrum began working as a part-time secretary at the company. She is involved in many different aspects of the business.

In September of 1996 Derrick Jennings was hired in the service department of the company. Today he continues to work in service and also helps with the delivery of propane.

In the competitive world of business as we know it today, the propane industry has changed dramatically over the years. Not only do we have to contend with the competition in the industry, we have to deal with the Federal Department of Transportation and the rules and regulations that they pass down each year. Mississippi also carries their own rules and regulations that we have to contend with. The expense of carrying insurance has quadrupled over the past year alone. The above factors have many people in the propane industry leery about the future of the continued success of small businesses.

Along with the propane and the delivery of propane, we have a well stocked showroom floor with the most updated appliances you will find in the industry. Among these you will find Ducane Gas Grills, Vanguard and Rinnai Heaters, Atlanta Gas Logs, Re-Verberray and Mr. Heaters, Fish Cookers, Bradford White and Reliance Hot Water Heaters and Buck Stove Gas Logs and Inserts.

Craig and Melissa continue to strive to give each customer the personal touch and individual attention that they deserve. Service is the main ingredient in a successful operation and we take pride in our efforts to serve the people of Chickasaw County.

NORMAN INSURANCE AGENCY, INC.

In 1949 Wallace Norman, Sr. and Leland Brown Norman, Sr. founded Norman Insurance Agency. At the time the office was located on the west side of the square in Houston above Horn's Grocery. With Leland working a full time job at the bank, Wallace handled most of the agency's business. Mrs. Louise Norman, Leland's wife, assisted them as their secretary. Some time later, Leland sold his interest in the agency to Wallace, and the name was changed to Wallace Norman Insurance Agency. Soon after, Wallace moved the agency to a building behind the Houston Post Office and then later moved again to Pearl Street where he owned and operated Norman Oil Company.

The agency has always been a family business. Maurene Collums Norman, Wallace's wife, got her agent's license and sold insurance through the agency as well. Maurene continued to work at the agency until her death in 1994. Dana Leigh Hathorn Norman also joined the agency after she married Wallace, Jr. in 1977, and is still working there today. Through the years several long-term employees have worked in the Wallace Norman Insurance Agency such as Faula Fant, Norma McAlpin, and Joyce Freeman. Gaye Booth is currently in her 12th year at the agency.

Together, Wallace and Maurene started giving away Bibles to individuals and churches in the early 1970s. Even today Wallace continues to give Bibles away at the agency. Both Wallace and Maurene felt that this was the best way to reach out to the community.

Wallace Norman Insurance Agency, Inc. is proud to have served the people of Chickasaw County for the past 53 years and looks forward to continued business in the community.

Lion Oil Truck owned by Wallace Norman, Sr. Children left to right: Wallace Jr., Karen and Emily. 1959

Picture of a fan advertising the Norman Insurance Agency from early days in Houston.

Norman Insurance building at its location today, 2002.

PARKS & PARKS WELL SERVICES, INC.

Rayburn Parks, Owner

Parks & Parks Water Well Services, Inc., located on Okolona Cut-off Rd. in Houston, was started in 1979 by brothers, Rayburn and Hubert Parks, and was jointly owned until Hubert's death in 1996. The two began with a building of 3500 square feet and three employees as water well contractors, offering drilling, sales and service. The business has since grown to occupy buildings totaling over 17,500 square feet and employs 45 people, including five full-time maintenance employees.

*Tommy Washington
Operations Manager*

Parks & Parks does municipal, industrial, and commercial drilling, concentrating on municipal water systems, drilling and servicing those systems, which are funded by government agencies. The business currently has five drilling rigs in service, as well as five service rigs. There is also a complete maching shop where they build their own pumps.

Janice Moore, Secretary

*Jayne Aycock, Office Manager
Christine Morrissy,
Computer Consultatnt*

*Machine Shop
Roger Smith, Machinist*

Demeka Martinez, Receptionist

PENICK FARM AND PRODUCE CO., INC.

In 1915 Herbert E. Penick and son John R. Penick moved to Vardaman, Mississippi, in a covered wagon from Martin, Tennessee, a distance of 200 miles. It took about eight days covering around 25 miles per day. The wagon was heavily loaded with hay, corn, plow tools, and seed sweet potatoes. Granddaddy Herbert had traded 40 acres of land in Martin, Tennessee, for 240 in Mississippi. A good way to increase their farming operation. This 240 acres is still in the family and 3,000 more have been added.

John Rotoun Penick

Four generations of potato farmers, from left: Herbert E. Penick, John Russell Penick, J.R. Penick, Jr. and Terrell Penick.

John R. Penick III

Granddaddy Herbert and Daddy weren't the first people to grow sweet potatoes in Mississippi because most farmers at that time grew what they needed for home use.

The Penick family claim to be the first farmers to ship sweet potatoes commercially which we are still doing today after 86 years.

I was born in 1925 and remember granddaddy had two sweet potato curing houses. One was made of logs and the other of pine lumber. They shipped some potatoes by rail, loaded in Vardaman. I remember trucks coming from Chicago when it was dry enough for trucks to travel on our dirt roads.

In the last three years we have built the latest curing and storage warehouse in the USA. It took granddaddy four to six weeks to cure potatoes; we now can cure them in five days, with automatic control heating, humidifier, and exhaust fans.

We have shipped potatoes to states of Oregon, Nebraska, Michigan, Pennsylvania, Oklahoma, Arkansas, North Carolina, Tennessee, Florida, Alabama and Louisiana. Our volume runs around 700 trailer loads per year which would be around 700,000 bushels.

By J.R. Penick, Jr.

This Page Compliments of

KEITH POUNDS, CPA

444 E. Madison Street
Houston, MS 38851
456-3334

Providing bookkeeping and tax services since 1983

REA'S COUNTRY LANE CONSTRUCTION, INC.
102 RHODES ST.   HOUSTON, MS 38851   662-456-9898

Rea's Country Lane Construction Co., Inc. was originally incorporated in 1983, by owners Oneal, Earline, Wayne and Joyce Rea. Since 1990 Wayne and Joyce Rae are current owners.

Looking south toward Houston, the old 'overpass bridge' for the OH & CC (Okolona, Houston and Calhoun City) railraod. In the late 1990s the bridge was removed, the cavity filled with dirt and Highway 15 resurfaced.

Houlka Creek Bridge, February 1915; occasion unknown.

THE PAGE SPONSORED BY REA'S COUNTRY LANE CONSTRUCTION CO. INC.

RADIO SHACK DEALER ASSOCIATE STORE

Original Radio Shack located at 689 North Jackson Street, Houston

Charles and Betty Moore have been in business at 689 and 685 North Jackson Street 25 years. In 1976 the Moores purchased the old Ford Equipment Building at 689 North Jackson Street from Mr. Willie Jim Linn. It took several weeks to give the building a face-lift. The north end of the building was rented as a mechanic shop to J.I. Lowery and his son, Ronnie, who was an artist and sign painter.

Originally the business began as Moore's This-N-That, with carpet, vinyl floor covering and home decorating items. Later a music department was created when guitars, PA systems, song books, how-to-play books, 45-records, car stereos, CBs and scanners were added to stock. Gospel sound tracks, wedding music, and recorded music also became available in the music department. In 1981 the old building was sold to Frank Smith's Body Shop and the Moores purchased the Radio Shack franchise.

Woodruff's Grocery Store, site of current Radio Shack building.

In 1976, the old Earl Woodruff Grocery Store and home, located next door at 685 North Jackson Street was purchased. Those buildings were removed and the present building was built, which now houses Moore Electronics, Radio Shack Dealer; and Nancy's Classy Cuts in the north end of the building; and Patsy's Beauty Shop in the south end of the building.

In 2001 the Radio Shack franchise was purchased by son, Gary and his wife Melissa. Gary and Melissa have one daughter, Laura Claire. Gary has expanded the business to include Quick-Pay bill payment services for approximately 60 companies, including BellSouth home phone bills, Cingular Wireless, Direct TV, Dish Network, and other public service utility bills and credit cards. A full line of Radio Shack items–car stereos and home surround sound systems, cellular service by Cingular Wireless, and pager service are offered.

Radio Shack Dealer Associate Store, today.

In 2002, Gary and Bro. Don Locke, a local pastor, formed a nonprofit organization and obtained a nonprofit FCC license for a Christian radio station to go on the air at 103.7 on the FM band. The station will be located upstairs above Radio Shack and will be airing American Family Radio affiliated-type programming, 24 hours daily.

WARE FARMS

This property located off Highway 15 near Chewawa Creek canal, has been in the Ware family for many years. We have records and information from family members proving this property was purchased from the Indians. We have an undated document, Deed of Conveyance patent from the U.S. Government to Te Wak Yea. The original deeds were destroyed by the Union Army in 1863.

George Washington "Wash" Ware was the owner of the property at the time of his death in 1862. He was killed at the Battle of Shiloh along with 10,500 others, in a two day battle under Commanders Johnson and Beauregard, April 6th and 7th, 1862, and was buried at Shiloh. His wife, Cassie Ann Turman Ware, and children, Nannie, Ed, George W. II and Simuel Ware, became heirs of the property. Cassie Ann died in 1899 and was buried at Bethel Baptist Church, Woodland, Mississippi.

Simuel Ware and his wife, Irania Cordelia Chapman "Delia" Ware, bought the property from the sisters and brothers and his mother, Cassie Ann, several years be-

fore she died. Delia was known throughout the community as a hard working woman. She had 12 children, Thomas, Floyd, Pascal, Allen, Mabel (Naron), Madel (Naron), Vera (Bryant), Corrine (Springer), Simmie (Andrews), Mason, George W. III, and Velma. She cooked for the whole family, plowed a mule, smoked, had red hair. Her husband died in 1910 at 55 years of age from pneumonia. She and her children worked hard to keep the land and provide for the family.

In 1947 Allen and Clytee, Barbara, Elizabeth, James and Frank Ware bought the property from the children and Delia. Delia died in 1954 at Houston Hospital after complications from surgery.

Allen Ware died in 1974 leaving the property to his wife, she sold it to Frank and Carolyn Ware in 1984. They are the owners at the present time. It is currently a cattle ranch. In the past it had many crops such as cotton, soybeans, corn and vegetables.

We have been blessed to have had this land for so many years in the family. God has allowed us to use this land and through good times and bad times, he has seen us through. Roots are very important, and we hope to pass this land on to our children, Dana Ware, Angela Ware (Mohr) and husband David, Richard Ware and wife Melissa, and our grandchildren Ricky Ware, David Chase Mohr, Kaddy Ware and Franklin Rivers Mohr.

Thanks to Vivian Sepulveda, daughter of Thomas Ware, for information and dates for this history. She too enjoyed living on this farm.

Researched and written by Carolyn Ware and Libba Criddle.

Simuel T. Ware

Delia Ware

WOODLAND WHOLESALE-RETAIL FURNITURE INC.
133 GRADY STREET   WOODLAND, MS 39776   662-456-4315

In 1958, during another school consolidation in Chickasaw County, the little school at Woodland was closed. Students were sent to Houston. Neighbors and former students of the school, Mr. Henry and "Ms. Jo" Bullard, decided to offer a bid for the property. To their surprise, they were the new owners of most of the Woodland school property.

It was suggested that a furniture store that would retail locally made products be located in the old school property. The idea was a good one and 16 years later, the store encompasses 450,000 square feet in several buildings.

Woodland Furniture is still family owned - in fact it has grown to be the largest family owned furniture store in the state of Mississippi.

WEAVER'S AUTO PARTS, INC.
CELEBRATES 20 YEARS OF SERVICE

J.B. Gammill, Jerry Weaver and Keith Lawrence, 1983.

Weaver's Auto Parts, Inc. is proud and honored to have served their customers of Chickasaw County and surrounding counties for the past 20 years. Jerry and Donna Weaver bought the NAPA Auto Parts Store from Carroll Sparks in January of 1983. Since then the business has more than quadrupled in sales and inventory.

There has been a NAPA Auto Parts store in Houston since 1949. First owned by Murray and Evelyn Cliett and was located on the southeast corner of the Square in Houston. Raymond and Lucille Rowland purchased the store from the Cliett's in 1952 and moved the store several times. After Raymond Rowland, Sr. passed away the store was owned and operated by Lucille and Raymond Rowland, Jr., located on W. Hamilton Street. In 1980 Carroll Sparks bought the store and in 1983 Jerry and Donna Weaver became the owners. The Weavers have moved the store twice which is now located at 318 W. Madison Street, Houston, Mississippi. Recently a 4,000 sq. ft. warehouse building was added at this location.

Weaver's Auto Parts, Inc. has been sponsors of the Spring Flywheel Festival and Tractor Pull for the past 12 years which has grown to be something the town looks forward to each year. They are also sponsors of the Houston High School Solar Car which took first place in the nation in 2001. Other organizations donated to include Boy Scouts of America, Houston Band Boosters, Houston High Touchdown Club, Houston High School Baseball program, Houston High School Annual Staff, P.A.C.E., The Pilot Club of Houston, Special Olympics, Make a Wish Foundation and The American Cancer Society.

Jerry and Donna Weaver wish to thank their customers and friends for helping to make Weaver's Auto Parts, Inc. successful. They look forward to being a part of the growth of Chickasaw County in the future.

Jason Womack, Jerry Weaver, Dona Weaver and Jesse Ward, 2002.

SHASCO INC.

June 15, 1974, Kenny Scott and Carl Rogers started a business called Professional Htg., & AC in the old Houston Dairy Building.

In 1977 the partnership split up. Carl operated Professional Htg. & AC and Kenny started a contracting business called Scott Heating and AC.

In 1978 we changed the name to Shasco Wholesale Supply and began to do wholesale business.

In 1981 we incorporated as Shasco Inc. and no longer did any contracting work. At this time we sold Scott Htg. & AC to Scott Criddle.

At the present time we have two locations - Houston and Louisville, Mississippi, and at the present time we have 15 employees.

Our primary business is heating and air conditioning equipment and supplies, water coolers, ice machines, industrial fans as well as a complete line of parts for heating and air conditioning and appliance parts.

Our territory is North Mississippi and West Alabama.

Pictured is our Shasco Inc. building, located at 1000 N. Jackson, and owners Kenny and Georgia Scott.

INDEX

Charlie Thomas and wife, Jadie Neal Thomas, with baby Charles Richard (Dick); Mary Evelyn Thomas Pate on left and Sarah Thomas Childs on right. Circa 1922.

Cousins Viva, Ruth, Cassie and Zelynn Hobson. Their mothers were sisters of the Bugg family.

George (Fate) Wooldridge and Mary Jessie Moore Wooldridge.

On Sunday, April 15, 1917, folks gathered at Enon Primitive Baptist Church to celebrate C. Edd Couch's 66th birthday. This was the first of the "Third Sunday in April Annual Singing and Dinner on the Ground" events, which have continued to the present. The United States had declared war on Germany only nine days earlier and if you look closely, you can see several boys in front holding flags.

*Logs making their way to the mill the old
fashioned way. Courthouse is in the
background.*

Bob and Pecolia Bailey and baby.

Lemuel A. Porter (1810-1880) and wife Louisa P. Gregory (1811-1862), parents of Saryann Elizabeth (Sally) Porter, wife of John Luke Davis.

FAMILY RECORD

NAME	BIRTH		DEATH	
	Date	Place	Date	Place

FAMILY RECORD

NAME	BIRTH		DEATH	
	Date	Place	Date	Place

FAMILY TREE

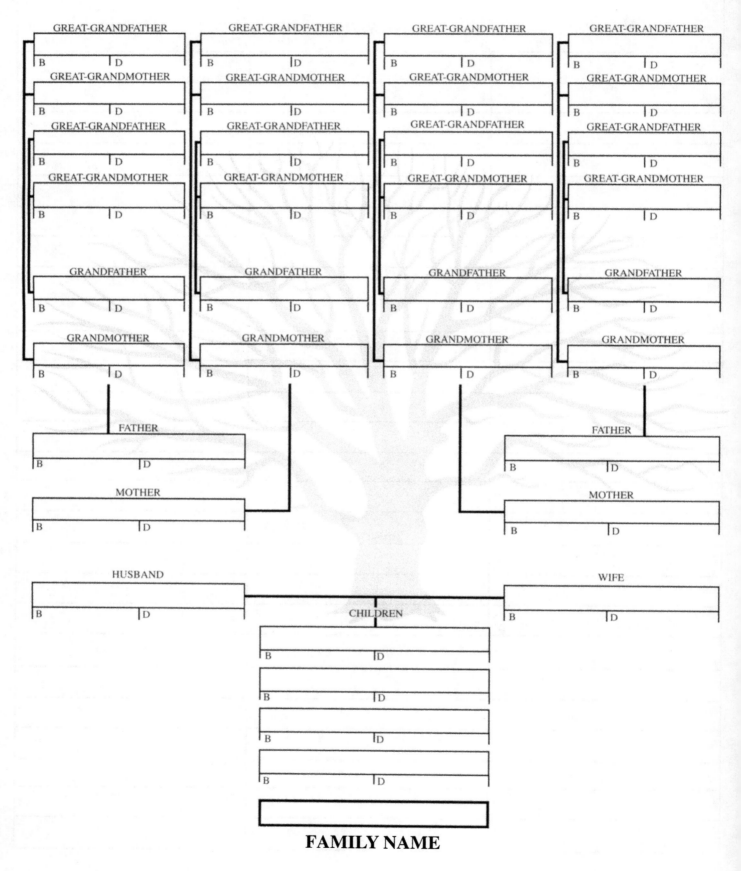

GREAT-GRANDFATHER

B | D

GREAT-GRANDMOTHER

B | D

GREAT-GRANDFATHER

B | D

GREAT-GRANDMOTHER

B | D

GREAT-GRANDFATHER

B | D

GREAT-GRANDMOTHER

B | D

GREAT-GRANDFATHER

B | D

GREAT-GRANDMOTHER

B | D

GREAT-GRANDFATHER

B | D

GREAT-GRANDMOTHER

B | D

GREAT-GRANDFATHER

B | D

GREAT-GRANDMOTHER

B | D

GREAT-GRANDFATHER

B | D

GREAT-GRANDMOTHER

B | D

GREAT-GRANDFATHER

B | D

GREAT-GRANDMOTHER

B | D

GRANDFATHER

B | D

GRANDMOTHER

B | D

GRANDFATHER

B | D

GRANDMOTHER

B | D

GRANDFATHER

B | D

GRANDMOTHER

B | D

GRANDFATHER

B | D

GRANDMOTHER

B | D

FATHER

B | D

MOTHER

B | D

FATHER

B | D

MOTHER

B | D

HUSBAND

B | D

WIFE

B | D

CHILDREN

B | D

B | D

B | D

B | D

FAMILY NAME

FAMILY TREE

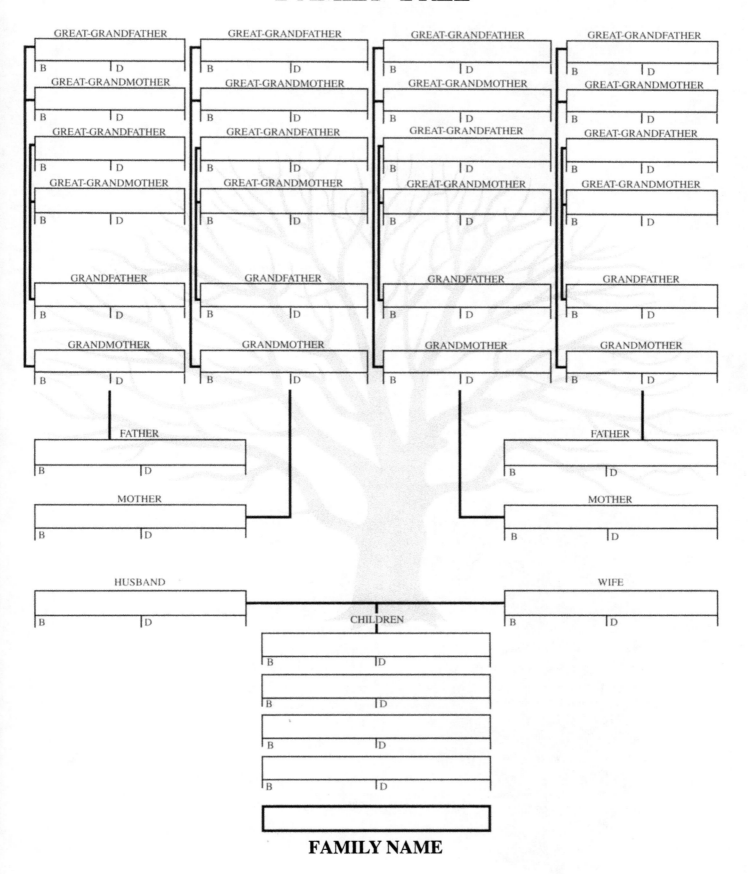

GREAT-GRANDFATHER
B | D

GREAT-GRANDMOTHER
B | D

GREAT-GRANDFATHER
B | D

GREAT-GRANDMOTHER
B | D

GREAT-GRANDFATHER
B | D

GREAT-GRANDMOTHER
B | D

GREAT-GRANDFATHER
B | D

GREAT-GRANDMOTHER
B | D

GREAT-GRANDFATHER
B | D

GREAT-GRANDMOTHER
B | D

GREAT-GRANDFATHER
B | D

GREAT-GRANDMOTHER
B | D

GREAT-GRANDFATHER
B | D

GREAT-GRANDMOTHER
B | D

GREAT-GRANDFATHER
B | D

GREAT-GRANDMOTHER
B | D

GRANDFATHER
B | D

GRANDFATHER
B | D

GRANDFATHER
B | D

GRANDFATHER
B | D

GRANDMOTHER
B | D

GRANDMOTHER
B | D

GRANDMOTHER
B | D

GRANDMOTHER
B | D

FATHER
B | D

MOTHER
B | D

FATHER
B | D

MOTHER
B | D

HUSBAND
B | D

WIFE
B | D

CHILDREN
B | D
B | D
B | D
B | D

FAMILY NAME

255

NOTES

Rice Stix factory and worker

Carter's Store, Van Vleet, MS in the early 1900s.

...ississippi, August 12, 1955.

Tabb Sawmill in Houston, MS, date unknown.